What Couples Are Saying About The Marriage Prayer

The format fits our busy lifestyle—small chunks, lots of illustrations that made us pause to share a laugh or a comment about topics we still deal with after thirty-five years of marriage. This book should be required reading for couples considering marriage, those recently married, and those of us who are still working on getting it right.

—Dave and Kathy, married thirty-five years

Finances are often a major point of contention in marriage, but rarely addressed by marriage book authors. We were happy to see that The Marriage Prayer *covered this important topic.*

—Josh and Karlene, married six years

We both found the format entertaining and engaging. The Marriage Prayer *is a very positive focal point. We liked the practical applications focusing on the emotional and spiritual health of our spouse.*

—Clark and Ann, married thirty-three years

The His and Her prayers are a great way to keep that commitment fresh in your mind, reminding you to give your best to your spouse every day!
—Colby and Renee, married seven years

We enjoyed the unique format of this book. The conversational writing style was easy to follow and the exercises helped us think about and apply the information presented.

—Johnny and Christy, married sixteen months

We've gained a new attitude and heart toward Jesus, each other, and anyone else, which came about from The Marriage Prayer ... *"Help me love You more than her/him, and her/him more than anyone or anything else."*

—Jeffrey and Julia, married seven years

We appreciated the examples, quizzes and practical applications suggested throughout the book. It does not matter how long you have been married, these suggestions are always helpful and a much need reminder that any marriage is a work in progress.

—Steve and Becky, married thirty years

I absolutely loved your Big Idea #6—"Marriage works well when we worship well." Ideas and thoughts jump off of the page wanting to be learned and implemented. We are looking forward to using this book in pre-marital and marriage counseling.

—Mike and Leslie, married thirty-two years

Every successful marriage needs the type of practical applications offered by The Marriage Prayer.

—Steve and Sue, married thirty-one years

THE
MARRIAGE PRAYER

PATRICK MORLEY
AND **DAVID DELK**

MOODY PUBLISHERS
CHICAGO

Editor: Jim Vincent
Cover Design: Levan Fisher Design
Cover Photos: © George Doyle & Ciarin Griffin/Stockbyte
Interior Design: Cathleen Kwas
All photographic images by iStock. Used by permission.

Library of Congress Cataloging-in-Publication Data

Morley, Patrick M.
  The marriage prayer : a prescription to change the direction of your marriage / Patrick Morley and David Delk.
     p. cm.
  ISBN 978-0-8024-7550-3
  1. Marriage—Religious aspects—Christianity. I. Delk, David. II. Title.
  BV835.M675 2008
  248.8'44--dc22

                    2008020248

We hope you enjoy this book from Moody Publishers. Our goal is to provide high-quality, thought-provoking books and products that connect truth to your real needs and challenges. For more information on other books and products written and produced from a biblical perspective, go to www.moodypublishers.com or write to:

Moody Publishers
820 N. LaSalle Boulevard
Chicago, IL 60610

1 3 5 7 9 10 8 6 4 2

Printed in the United States of America

Pat dedicates this book to the marriages of his daughter, Jen, and husband, Jay, and to his son, John, and wife, Kristie. And also to the memory of his father, Bob, and his mother, Alleen, who had a beautiful 54 year marriage. They lived for each other. Both passed away in 2002 within a few weeks of each other and went to be with Jesus.

David (and his wife Ruthie) dedicate this book to couples all across the country who, when facing devastating sin and difficult circumstances, are choosing to stay the course. A few of you have shared your story with us. You are our heroes.

Acknowledgments

All books are the products of many authors, but none more so than this.

A special thanks to Ruthie Delk for the Herculean effort you put forth. This book is **so** much better because you were involved. Thanks also to Ryan, Sarah, and Kyle for patience with early mornings, late nights, and more than one Saturday morning.

Thanks to Cathleen Kwas for infinite creativity and unlimited patience—a rare combination. Your work on design and layout is amazing.

We are grateful to work with a tremendous staff at Man in the Mirror. Many of them heard the concepts in this book being taught, while others gave their feedback on the manuscript. You all are amazing: Pam Adkins, Jim Angelakos, Ruth Cameron, Sharon Carey, Bernie Clark, Brett Clemmer, Will Fox, Joanne Hunt, Vanessa Jones, Donna Keiderling, Kelly Laughridge, Michael Lenahan, Stephanie Lopez, Liz Luke, Michael Maine, Daphne Mayer, Scott Russell, Tracie Searles, Jim Seibert, Jamie Smith, Antonio Stevens, Svana Tolf, Greg Wilkinson, and Rise Wilson.

At the risk of forgetting a few, we'd also like to thank all the couples who shared their stories and/or field-tested the book (in no particular order): Glen and Kimberly, Steve and Sue, Chuck and Linda, Dan and Alisa, Clark and Ann, Steve and Becky, Charles and Kim, Jay and Becky, Ken and Lee, Mike and Michelle, Chris and Lorraine, Scott and Pam, John and Angie, Steve and Sue, Jeffrey and Julia, Mike and Leslie, Robert and Kitty, Lyle and Marge, Bill and Beth, Robert and Sarah, Mike and Holly, Lance and Sonya, David and Lynn, Craig and Leigh, Rod and Judy, John and Lori, Keith and Lisa, Fred and Deb, Tony and Pat, Josh and Karlene, David and Karen, and Colby and Renee.

In addition, we are so grateful to work with a wonderful team at Moody Publishers— Janis Backing, Dave DeWit, John Hinkley, Holly Kisly, Paul Santhouse, Greg Thornton, and Jim Vincent.

Thanks so much to Robert Wolgemuth, Erik Wolgemuth, and Andrew Wolgemuth, for the great work they do as our representatives.

Thanks also to the men and women who open their lives to us week by week—it's a great privilege to walk this journey with you.

Table of Contents

Section 1—Faithfulness

I said, "'Til death do us part"—I want to mean it.

Section 2—Priorities

Help me love You more than her, and her more than anyone or anything else.

Section 3—Purpose

Help me bring her into Your presence today.

Section 4—Unity
Make us one, like You are three in one.

Section 5—Attitude
I want to hear her, cherish her, and serve her.

Section 6—Goal
So she would love You more and we can bring You glory.

This Book

...ent from most other books at the book-
...t to think about it.

...ok on relationships. Yes, it has a lot of
...about marriage, but it's presented in a

...few years on how people learn. There's
...eads to changes in behavior.

...thing it sees.

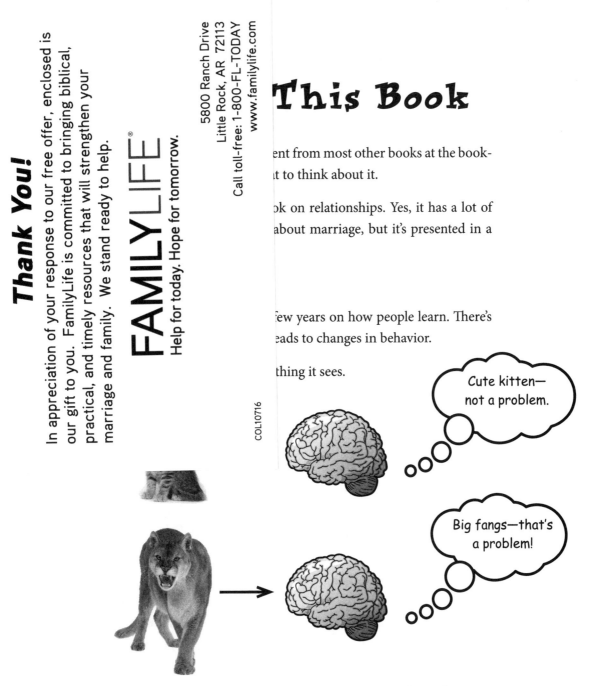

> Cute kitten—
> not a problem.

> Big fangs—that's
> a problem!

Your brain automatically helps you by keeping low-priority items from cluttering your thinking. Unfortunately, studies show that the text of traditional books is usually treated as low-priority by your mind. It's really difficult to overcome the fact that your brain says boring, old text just must not be that important. That means you have to work extra hard to learn and apply information presented in the traditional way.

So we decided to do something different. We've used this research to design this book for maximum impact. We wanted you to not only understand the ideas in the book, but also put them into action. We learned what kicks your brain into gear and designed the book based on these ideas.

What are the key design features we use and why are they important?

We integrate images to communicate ideas.

Studies have shown that images lead to up to 89 percent improvement in recall and transfer. We want the ideas in this book to be *understandable* and *memorable*. You'll also see that the graphics we've included are not just added to the book. **They're as much a part of the "text" as the text.**

We help you to think—really think.

We try to *motivate, encourage, chide, cajole*—and several other verbs—to get you to really consider how these ideas apply to your life. That's the whole purpose, right? But we keep it fun. You'll find discussion questions, puzzles, fill-in-the-blank, rating scales, and other activities all designed **to take your reading beyond the surface.**

We write in a conversational style.

If you're an English professor, watch out. Some of our sentences in this book aren't complete. Like this. That's because studies show up to **40 percent better retention** from a *conversational tone* than formal writing. So we tell *stories* instead of *lecture*. And while we take the subject of marriage very seriously, we try not to take ourselves too seriously.

We use true stories.

People learn best from seeing how real people deal with real problems. We had some great couples open their lives to us so we could tell you their stories. We know some of these will echo your experience in ways that are rich and real.

We've made the applications believable and achievable.

You'll notice a bunch of tiny, bite-sized "next steps" in this book (like the sample "connection point" below). That's because we know that *if we can get you moving* in the right direction, chances are *you will keep moving.* And if you need to turn around from where you are headed now, **it's a lot easier to do that with a small step than with a giant leap**.

> **Connection Point**
>
> How much honesty is there in your communication today compared to five years ago?
>
> Him:
>
> | Much Less Honesty | Less Honesty | More Honesty | Much More Honesty |
>
> Her:
>
> | Much Less Honesty | Less Honesty | More Honesty | Much More Honesty |

We write so you can discuss this book with other couples

You'll find many places in the book where we ask you to share your thoughts with your spouse, and then with a group. If possible, find some friends and work through this book together. Life's too short to go it alone. If you're a group leader, be sure to check out our Leader's Guide at the back of the book.

We speak to your heart.

We know that you'll **remember and act on things that you care about**. So we speak to your emotions—with *humor*, elements of *surprise*, appeals to your *curiosity*, and *stories* of real people.

We know change isn't easy.

There are no formulas for a perfect marriage. The Marriage Prayer isn't a mantra you can repeat to make everything turn out okay. We offer this book as a part of the process of change that God wants to work in your heart.

We include Scripture.

The best writing and insights in the world have no inherent power to change a human heart. God promises His word will transform lives. So most of the time when we reference a verse we include the entire text as well. If you skip some stuff in this book, don't skip the Scripture.

In addition, this material has been taught on numerous occasions to groups of men and women, and we also had groups field-test the presentation. They helped us refine the content and the layout so that it will be more effective for you. We are grateful to our publishers for being willing to experiment with something new and different.

By the way, you and your spouse can share this book. We'll ask you to grab some scratch paper a few times, but other than that it won't be a problem. We hope you enjoy the new format, but more than that, we pray God will use it to help grow your marriage.

Finally, we also owe a debt of gratitude to Kathy Sierra and Bert Bates, the creators of the Head First series of books. The lessons learned from these leaders informed much of the learning theory we have implemented in this book.

We've had a blast working on this book. It's been great to talk to so many couples and hear all that God has done in their lives. We consider it a privilege that you are investing your time and energy to have a better marriage! It's a joy to be on the journey with you. Thanks for reading, and may God bless your marriage.

Introducing The Marriage Prayer

We've been working with people—especially men—for a long time at Man in the Mirror. Men struggle with a lot of things. But if we were to take the marriage issue and put it on one side of the scale, and take all of the other problems men deal with and put them on the other side, the marriage issue would outweigh all the others combined. By a ton.

We live in a fallen world, and marriages are often not working the way God planned.

When it's going good, marriage can be the best thing in the world. There is no greater joy than experiencing the unadulterated love of another person.

When it's going bad, marriage can be horrible.

Another Book on Marriage?

I hate to be mean, but do we really need another Christian book on marriage?

Yeah—Have you been to a book-store lately? Hasn't everything already been written?

That's a fair question. And our answer is, basically, yes.

So why would we write this book? If our goal was to compile more information about marriage, we wouldn't have. But that's not our goal. If you're like most of us, you probably already *know* a lot more about relationships than you actually *do*.

When you know a lot more than you do in a marriage, you end up like most people in a "get along" marriage. They're getting along. These are not bad marriages, they're good…but they're not great. These marriages are a pale shadow of the full potential we see in the Scriptures for a thriving marriage.

How do you build a thriving marriage? We've found consistently over the years that people end up doing what they really want to do. So one of the first steps in building a thriving marriage is to **want** to build one. Our desires change not so much based on what we know, but more often based on what we **believe**. So we hope to help you really believe some things about marriage, God, your spouse, real love, Jesus, and the love and forgiveness God has for you.

I get it! What I **believe** will eventually influence what I **want** and then what I **do**.

Exactly. That's what *The Marriage Prayer* is all about.

This book is different from any marriage book we've ever seen. It's not so much a book as it is a user's guide. If it's tough to put together a bookshelf without the directions, why should we think we can build a marriage?

The one main idea that permeates this book is this—your relationship will improve dramatically if you start to pray a prayer every day that summarizes what you hope for in your marriage.

The applications come every few pages in bite-sized pieces that you can actually do.

Our goal is to motivate, encourage, and help you take real steps to a better marriage. We've worked really hard to make things biblical, simple, believable, and compelling.

We pray God will use our words to change your mind, your heart, your behavior, and your marriage—for His glory.

The Marriage Prayer

The first step we would suggest to improve your marriage is to begin praying The Marriage Prayer every day. The text of this prayer summarizes a biblical view of marriage. In the rest of the book, we'll walk through each of the concepts and draw lots of practical applications.

Start right now by reading the prayer on the next page, then say it as a prayer to God. Hopefully, as you continue through the book, the prayer will come to mean more and more to you every day.

Guys, this one's for us. Remember, pray it every day.

The Marriage Prayer—For Him

Father,

I said, "'Til death do us part"—I want to mean it.

Help me love You more than her,

       and her more than anyone or anything else.

Help me bring her into Your presence today.

Make us one, like You are three in one.

I want to hear her, cherish her, and serve her—

So she would love You more and we can bring You glory.

Amen

Ladies, here's ours. Pray it daily for your husband.

The Marriage Prayer—For Her

Father,

I said, "'Til death do us part"—I want to mean it.

Help me love You more than him,

       and him more than anyone or anything else.

Help me bring him into Your presence today.

Make us one, like You are three in one.

I want to hear him, support him, and serve him—

So he would love You more and we can bring You glory.

Amen

Section 1: Faithfulness

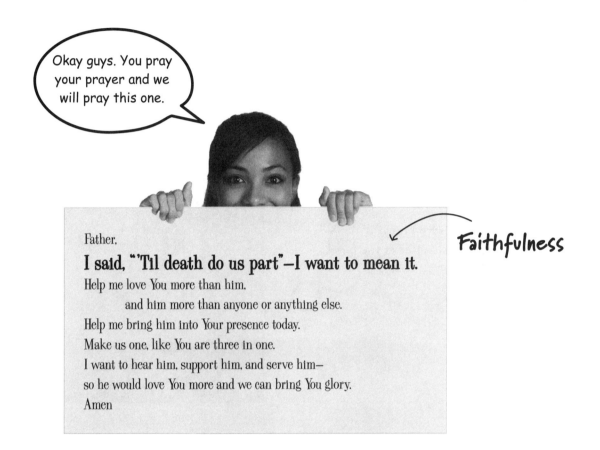

Okay guys. You pray your prayer and we will pray this one.

Father,

I said, "'Til death do us part"—I want to mean it.

Help me love You more than him,

and him more than anyone or anything else.

Help me bring him into Your presence today.

Make us one, like You are three in one.

I want to hear him, support him, and serve him—

so he would love You more and we can bring You glory.

Amen

Faithfulness

The next two chapters are about FAITHFULNESS. It can be a daunting thing to realize that marriage is forever.

Our culture has certainly lost this perspective—often death is not the thing doing the parting anymore; a lot of other things are. But you're reading this book because you want to be faithful to your spouse and to God.

In the next two chapters, we'll examine two big ideas:

▸ **After God, but before all others, make your spouse your top priority.**

▸ **It is God's will for this marriage to work.**

These chapters will give you practical ideas and proven steps to build security and deal with difficult times.

But we can't be faithful to our spouse in our own strength—that's why it's part of The Marriage Prayer. Begin each day asking God for continued faithfulness: "Father, I said 'Til death do us part'—I want to mean it…"

1: Security

Helping Your Spouse Feel Safe in Your Love

Throughout this book you'll find short exercises to do. We promise they won't take long. Even if you are the type who never does these things, PLEASE DO THEM. Just this once, okay? We'd say "please" one more time, but we don't want to start the book by annoying you. Here's the deal—if you're going to read this book anyway, you may as well add 10 percent more effort and get two or three times the benefit. (Besides, your spouse will really appreciate your making the extra effort.)

Think back to the days after you met your spouse. What was it like when you finally realized this was the person for you? As you remember how you felt, what are the first words that come to mind?

Him

❑ Ecstatic	❑ Scared	❑ Thrilled	❑ Relieved
❑ Nervous	❑ Loved	❑ Cautious	❑ Excited
❑ Pressured	❑ Other _____	❑ Other _____	

Her

❑ Ecstatic	❑ Scared	❑ Thrilled	❑ Relieved
❑ Nervous	❑ Loved	❑ Cautious	❑ Giddy
❑ Secure	❑ Other _____	❑ Other _____	

RULES OF ENGAGEMENT

Take no more than five minutes to discuss the words you chose. (We want you to be willing to do the exercises later.) What surprises you about your spouse's choices?

A (Slightly Disguised) True Story about...
Security and Significance
Justin and Erin

Erin (walking in door at night after a Brownie leadership meeting): "Hey honey—how was your meeting tonight?"

Justin (watching TV in the living room): "Good."

Erin: "What did they serve for your dinner?"

Justin: "Uhh...prime rib."

A pretty ordinary exchange, right? **Except that Erin already knew that the Contractors' Association dinner meeting _was actually next week_.**

Yesterday, she'd asked Justin if he could pick up their daughter from a friend's house after work. He'd told her the meeting for his new association was that night. She made other arrangements.

When he found out the next day that he didn't have the meeting, he didn't call Erin. She went online during the day and found out the real date.

Neither of them said anything more that night after their brief exchange. Then, at about two in the morning, Erin rolled over and punched Justin in the shoulder. "I checked online and I know you didn't have your meeting tonight, you big jerk."

To be continued...

Sound familiar? Stuffing something rather than talking about it?

How long has it been since you listened to a story around a campfire? Last year? Twenty years ago? No matter how long it's been, there's just something magical about hearing an interesting tale around a crackling fire.

Imagine what it would have been like thousands of years ago sitting around a fire at night with the Israelites. Since that was an oral culture, those times together would have been treasured and valued. When Moses told how the world began, you would have heard him say five times, "It was good." Then a sixth time he says, "It was very good."

Can you picture it in your mind? "It was good...It was good...It was good...It was good...It was good...It was very good."

After all that, it would have been quite a shock when you finally heard—"It is not good..." What isn't good? "The Lord God said, 'It is not good for the man to be alone'" (Genesis 2:18). In other words, the whole creation was good—everything— but it was not yet complete, because man did not have woman.

You and your spouse were literally made for each other.

 Have you ever gotten down to the last piece of a jigsaw puzzle and realized you couldn't find the last piece? You look and look but it's nowhere to be found. Then, as a last resort, you move the sofa and there it is.

Finding your spouse is like finding that final piece. There's a "rightness" that every human being longs to experience.

*Did you read the introduction? If not, **PLEASE READ IT NOW**. It's really important. We tell you why we give you lots of small action steps in this book. (They'll help your marriage—we promise.)*

PLEASE DO TRY THIS AT HOME

What's one way that you know your spouse was made for you? Is there a characteristic about them that "just fits"? Share that characteristic with your spouse and why you appreciate it.

Finding the one God gave you to spend your life with brings a powerful sense of security. You know that whatever else life might bring, there's one person who will always be right there with you. God said "It was not good…" because we need this sense of security that comes from real relationships, particularly within marriage.

Where Security Comes From

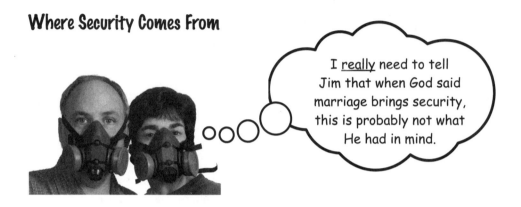

I _really_ need to tell Jim that when God said marriage brings security, this is probably not what He had in mind.

If you've been married more than a few months, you know that the wonderful rush of those first heady days often doesn't last. If you've been married a few years, you've probably slogged through dirty diapers, sales contests at work, or rushed dinners as you both run different directions. If you've been married a decade, you've likely had a first house, church committees, and trips to the emergency room.

It's easy in the honeymoon phase, when everything we do is right. But how are we supposed to find and provide security for the long term in our marriage?

Physically, we feel secure when we are in a safe place. We need to feel protected. We need to have our basic needs met—for food, clothing, and shelter.

It's the same way relationally. We feel secure in a relationship when we feel safe and we know that our needs are being met. Security comes when we are loved unconditionally by another person. Security comes when we know that it really is "'til death do us part." But relationally, security also comes when we _give_ as well as _get_, so part of feeling secure is being able to serve and meet the needs of our spouse. That's what we'll talk about in the rest of this chapter—how you **get** security in marriage and how you can **give** security to your spouse.

God gives us marriage for mutual support and encouragement. It's meant to be a safe harbor of love and respect. **But if we don't feel secure in our marriage, we'll spend all of our time worrying about that and none of our time growing and developing into the person God wants us to be.** So it's important to be secure; but it's also important to create security for our spouses so they can grow as well. In order to make it until "'til death do us part," you need to help your spouse feel secure. To do that, you need to understand how to help them meet their greatest needs.

A (Slightly Disguised) True Story about…
Security and Significance
Justin and Erin (continued)

After she punched Justin, Erin's next reaction was to tell him **she** *was sorry. She felt bad that she hadn't told him she knew his meeting was changed. She was afraid he would be angry that she was checking up on him. This was a holdover from a pattern that dominated the early years of their relationship.*

A lack of security…

Both Erin and Justin carried a lot of destructive habits into their marriage. Neither of them grew up in a Christian home, and they weren't Christians until after they had been married for several years.

As a young man, Justin drank after work and occasionally ended up visiting topless bars. For many years into his marriage, several times each month he turned his cell phone off after work and then finally arrived home after midnight.

A lack of security…

Erin just hoped this kind of behavior would go away. She couldn't tell anyone—she didn't want to make Justin or herself look bad. They had no friends they could open up with; she certainly couldn't tell anyone in their families.

A lack of security...

When he stumbled in late one night, she met him at the door in tears. "Why do you treat me this way? I would never do this to you!" Justin's response was his standard—"Can we talk about this tomorrow?"

Justin knew deep down that he was wrong, but he didn't want to admit it. He felt like a failure as a husband and as a man. He protected his self-image by getting angry and forcing Erin to back down.

To be continued…

A Man's Greatest Need

What do men want? We think you can boil it down to three things.

1. We want something we can give our lives to—**a cause**.

2. We want someone to share it with—**a companion**.

3. We want a reasonable explanation for why number one and number two are so difficult—**a conviction**.

That's right. Men need to give themselves to a cause that makes sense.

Men want to be significant. They want to do something with their lives. When a man finds a place of significance he feels secure. He knows that this is how God has wired him to be.

Even men without a lot of ambition or motivation want it to matter that they have lived. The trouble comes when a man finds himself consistently blocked from satisfying this desire to be significant. Often, these men go into a funk that affects everyone and everything around them. Perhaps that's happened to you.

ASK YOUR HUSBAND...

(Wife, read these questions to your husband.)

Do you agree that most men want a cause, a companion, and a conviction? How would you say this in your own words?

A Woman's Greatest Need

After God said, "It is not good for man to be alone," what did He say?

"I will make a helper suitable for him" (Genesis 2:18). The woman was made by God to be a companion in relationships. Men need a female companion, and females need a male companion.

A woman is designed to be a companion, a nurturer, and a helper. That doesn't mean a husband doesn't help his wife, but her basic nature is that she wants to be a companion, she wants to satisfy the "aloneness" that men feel. She's made to desire that connection with a man.

One way of talking about a woman's greatest need is to say that she wants **intimacy**. *Intimacy* means to be known, accepted, and loved at the deepest level of who she is.

Does she want to do something significant with her life? Does she want a cause? Does she want a mission? Of course! But even more than that, she longs for her husband to know and treasure her for who she really is.

ASk YouR WIFE...

(Husband, read these questions to your wife.)

Do you agree that a woman's greatest need is for intimacy? How would you say this in your own words?

A man was made for significance. A woman was made for intimacy. So the Scripture tells the wife to respect the husband (significance), and the husband to love the wife (intimacy). "However, each one of you also must love his wife as he loves himself, and the wife must respect her husband" (Ephesians 5:33).

Here are some other ways to understand how men and women typically find security. (Of course these are generalizations, and they don't hold true for every single man and woman. But they are generalizations because they do apply to most people to some degree. So, just because they are not always true, don't discount the fact that they are usually true.)

	Man	**Woman**
Greatest need:	significance	intimacy
Principal drive:	to be respected	to be cherished
Orientation:	to task	to relationship
Principal activity:	providing	nurturing
Direction of creativity:	work	home
Deepest fear:	failure to provide	losing a spouse or child
Risk-orientation:	taking risks	seeking security
Principal concerns:	money and meaning	husband and children

NBAS (No-Brainer Action Step)

Tell your spouse which line of the chart fits you best. Which words on the chart would you change?

Making Your Marriage a Safe Place

Security becomes the foundation for everything else God wants to accomplish in your marriage. If you or your spouse doesn't feel safe in your relationship, you won't be able to have a vibrant marriage. Instead of being able to serve your spouse and help them grow, you'll be hung up trying to have your own needs met.

Security must first of all come from Christ, not your spouse. Jesus promises to give you everything you really need. "Preach the gospel" to yourself every day. What does that mean? It means that you need to help yourself remember that you are perfectly loved and accepted by God. Jesus protects and guarantees your eternal security. "My sheep listen to my voice; I know them, and they follow me. I give them eternal life, and they shall never perish; no one can snatch them out of my hand. My Father, who has given them to me, is greater than all; no one can snatch them out of my Father's hand" (John 10:27–29).

> ### Our security in Christ flourishes when we realize:
>
> ■ we can abandon ourselves to His grace and
>
> ■ we can risk everything for His glory.

The gospel gives us the radical freedom to forget about ourselves because we know our ultimate needs will be met. We're like a person who can jump confidently from a cliff because he's wearing a safety harness, rope, bungee cord, and a parachute, with a giant air bag waiting at the bottom.

In contrast, if we don't get our security from Jesus first, then we'll place a burden on our spouse that they were never meant to bear. They simply cannot meet our deepest needs.

It's the difference between a vacuum cleaner and a hair dryer.

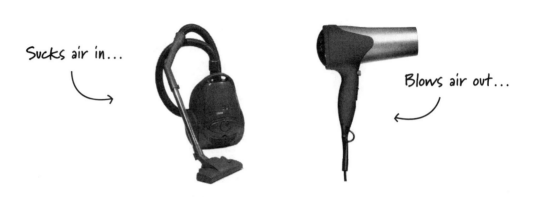

Sucks air in...

Blows air out...

No security in Christ = you try to suck meaning from the people around you, and it sucks the life from them. You're like a relational vacuum cleaner.

Security in Christ = you are living out of the overflow of Christ's love, so you can "blow" His love to others, like a relational hairdryer.

Connection Point

For both of you: Rate yourself on this scale:

Him: vacuum cleaner   hair dryer

Her: vacuum cleaner   hair dryer

How does this affect your marriage?

How to Give Your Spouse Security

The BIG Idea:

After God, but before all others, make your spouse your top priority.

God gave you your spouse to be your first responsibility. After your relationship with Him, the most important thing is to help your spouse become all God wants him or her to be. When your spouse knows they are the most important person in your life, they will have security.

When we pray, "I said ''til death do us part'—I want to mean it," we are asking God to help us be faithful. If you make your spouse the most important priority in your life after God, faithfulness will follow. The rest of this book will show you practical ways to make your spouse your top priority.

WAIT! You can't leave me hanging. How can I help my husband find significance in our marriage?

You're right. That would be cruel. We'll cover a lot more later, but here are a few practical ideas to help a man find security.

- **Encourage him in tasks that have an impact.** What is something your husband is involved in that makes a difference? If you can't think of anything, encourage him to find an outlet—such as helping with a sports team, assisting in a class at church, or chaperoning a Boy Scout outing. If he's already involved, ask how you can join him. One friend finally realized coaching baseball was great for her husband. Instead of resenting it, now she is the team mom.

- **Show appreciation for the things he does.** Everyone needs encouragement. Your husband has a lot of pressures and demands on his time and attention. Let him know how much you appreciate his earning an income, fathering your children, and being your husband.

- **Help him find opportunities for success with you, the children, and others.** Set him up to succeed, not to fail. Small choices with positive results lead to more good choices and more positive results. Encourage him to take a short walk with you, to say a prayer with the kids before bed, or to talk over the sermon with the family at Sunday lunch.

- **Clearly communicate your needs.** Most husbands want to do a good job. But a husband can't read his wife's mind. Tell him how to serve you so he can succeed.

- **Minimize criticism that belittles or degrades.** Nagging gets you nowhere in the long run. If your husband is not living strong, it's probably because he's insecure and unsure of what to do. Belittling and criticizing only digs the hole deeper.

Implement one of these ideas today and see how God uses it in your relationship.

Helloooo!!! If you're gonna help the ladies, the least you could do is give us a few ideas as well!

You're right. Again, that's pretty much what the rest of the book is about, but here are a few ideas to help you provide intimacy to your wife.

- **Stay connected with her emotionally.** Your wife wants you to understand how she feels, and she wants to know what is going on in your heart and mind as well. Take a moment today and talk with her about one substantive thing going on in your life. God cares so much about this that He instructed the newlywed husband to invest a year in nothing but the happiness of his wife—"he is to be free to stay at home and bring happiness to the wife he has married" (Deuteronomy 24:5).

- **Avoid criticism that threatens her sense of self.** Your wife faces a lot of pressure from our culture, her relationships, and her own self-image. She needs to know that you love her for who she is in spite of what she does or doesn't do. Tell her today that you love her no matter what.

- **Talk to her and pray with her.** Communication is a key to creating intimacy with your wife. Make time every day to have meaningful interaction. Ask questions about her day. Say The Marriage Prayer with her before you go to bed tonight. Look her in the eyes, ask how she's doing, and really listen to her answer.

A (Slightly Disguised) True Story about…
Security and Significance
Justin and Erin (continued)

Erin had spent years feeling unloved and unappreciated. She had the responsibility for the home and kids while Justin had the freedom to do whatever he wanted to do. But she never had the courage to really confront Justin.

Finally, Erin and Justin got involved in a small group with their church. After a few years of sitting in their leader's home and talking with their group, they came to realize that these people really cared about them. Due to some crises going on with other group members, they finally felt comfortable sharing their own story.

Over the next few months they grew in their understanding of God's love for them and their love for one another. Justin began to see how he should respect his wife and find his joy in their family. Erin finally felt secure enough to express her feelings to Justin without backing down and blaming herself.

Security in the love of Christ and in their love for one another...

Now they spend more time together as a family and are integrally involved in the life of their church. Their experience with Christ has transformed their marriage.

But like all of us, they're still a work in progress, Guess what? This story isn't an episode from years past—it happened only a few months ago. The difference this time? The episode ended with them talking and laughing in the middle of the night. That's progress.

Another Really Big Idea: The Emotional Bank Account

Every human being has what we might call an emotional bank account. Every interaction with your spouse is either a deposit or a withdrawal.

If you ignore your spouse when they are talking to you and continue reading or watching TV, that's a withdrawal. If you bring breakfast in bed, that's a deposit.

One way to help your spouse have security in your relationship is to make more deposits than withdrawals.

Every human being banks somewhere. Each person has emotional needs, and they attempt to have them met. If you don't fill these needs for your spouse, chances are that somebody else will. So be sure to memorize your spouse's account number. (And if you've forgotten it, ask your spouse—they'll be more than happy to remind you. ☺)

A Solid Foundation

Finding and providing security in your marriage relationship becomes a solid foundation for everything God wants to do in and through you individually and as a couple. Praying The Marriage Prayer can help you remember that your spouse is a gift to be treasured from God. When we pray in faith, He will answer and give us hearts to love Him and our spouse. When we make our spouse our top priority after God, we ultimately find the joy our hearts desire as well.

CHAPTER REVIEW

Using what you learned in this chapter, choose the correct answers for the multiple choice questions below. Give yourself 50 points for each correct answer.

1. In terms of relationships, you are either a...
   a. Pisces or Leo
   b. hair dryer or vacuum cleaner
   c. lizard tail or monkey foot

2. One of a man's greatest needs is...
   a. a remote control
   b. tickets to local revival of *Les Miserables*
   c. significance

3. One of a woman's greatest needs is...
   a. a bathrobe made from Peruvian yak fur
   b. intimacy
   c. Chanel #5

4. A key to providing security is to remember that your spouse has...
   a. flat feet
   b. a large handgun in the closet
   c. an emotional bank account

You Haven't Finished This Chapter Until...

We've got big hopes and dreams for this book. We've been planning, working, and praying so that God could use it to help your marriage. But He can't help you if you aren't open to Him really working in your life.

So, don't go on to the next chapter until...

❑ You've done all the exercises, including the Please Do Try This at Home (p. 21), No-Brainer Action Step (p. 27), the Connection Point (p. 28) and the sections

❑ Ask Your Spouse (pp. 25 and 26).

❑ You've begun saying The Marriage Prayer every day so that it is becoming a habit.

❑ Together, you've talked through the reflection questions (see below) either alone or with your group.

Questions for Reflection and Discussion

Use the questions to cement the ideas from this chapter into your marriage. Discuss them with your spouse and your small group of couples.

1. Is security an issue that you really struggle with? Why or why not?

2. What parts of Justin and Erin's "A True Story" in this chapter could you relate to? What aspects seemed foreign to you? What lessons could you learn from it for your marriage?

3. Does the big idea from this chapter resonate with you? Would your spouse say that they are your top priority after God?

4. What is one practical take-away you garnered from this chapter that you will implement in the next week? How will you do it?

2: Difficult Days

Sticking Together in Hard Times

All of us experience difficult times. Pick one of the following that has been a source of difficulty for you in the past. Remember, this is a quick exercise—so make it snappy.

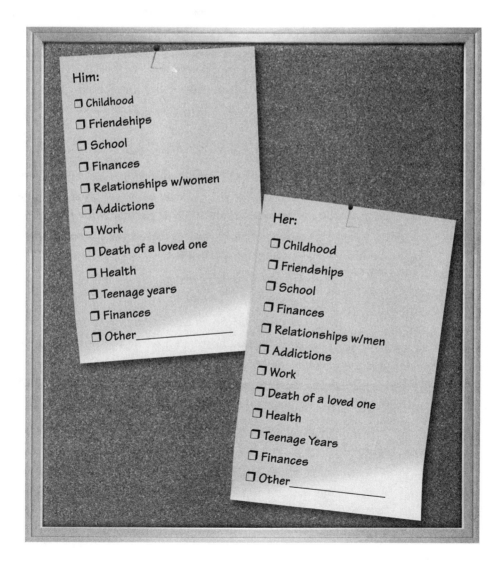

Him:
- ☐ Childhood
- ☐ Friendships
- ☐ School
- ☐ Finances
- ☐ Relationships w/women
- ☐ Addictions
- ☐ Work
- ☐ Death of a loved one
- ☐ Health
- ☐ Teenage years
- ☐ Finances
- ☐ Other_____

Her:
- ☐ Childhood
- ☐ Friendships
- ☐ School
- ☐ Finances
- ☐ Relationships w/men
- ☐ Addictions
- ☐ Work
- ☐ Death of a loved one
- ☐ Health
- ☐ Teenage Years
- ☐ Finances
- ☐ Other_____

RULES OF ENGAGEMENT

Discuss your answers briefly with your spouse (just trying to keep the process going). What made the situation difficult? How did you handle it at the time? What are one or two lessons you learned because of what you experienced?

A (Slightly Disguised) True Story about…Difficult Days
Michael and Amy

As Michael sat down for dinner with his family, he happened to glance at his wife, Amy, at the other end of the table. Something was different. Not a haircut. He was smart enough not to go the "Have you lost weight?" route. Then he glanced at her hands. He did a double take and looked again. "Where are your wedding rings?"

Amy looked at her hand, then back to Michael. "I sold them the other day. We need the money to pay the mortgage."

At the time, Michael had been out of work for a few months. They'd already sold the classic Mustang he'd restored, and Amy had been frustrated that he wasn't more aggressive in trying to find work. He'd already been through a number of jobs, but nothing ever seemed to last beyond a couple of years. She was stuck working full-time, then dealing with bills and creditors. So, half for the money and half out of spite, she went to a pawn shop with their twelve-year-old daughter and sold her wedding rings.

Can you identify with what they're feeling?

When Michael heard the news, he felt like a failure—both as a provider and as a husband. How could she make a decision like that without even talking to me?

To be continued…

In a few minutes you'll probably be wondering why we would make a discussion of difficult marriages the second chapter in the book. Seems like a downer, right?

YIPPEE—let's talk about having a miserable marriage right at the beginning of a Christian book on marriage.

Actually, we're using the principle of triage—take the most important cases first. If you're reading this book to make a good marriage better, or an average marriage good, it won't hurt you to read this chapter now.

But if you're reading this book and the papers are waiting to be signed at the lawyer's office, you may not make it through another chapter. For some people, reading this book is their last chance at staying together.

So if your marriage is rockin' along—fine. You may need this chapter someday for yourself. And perhaps you can use it right now to help a friend. But if your marriage is on the rocks—we wanted to get this chapter to you right away.

You Probably Know that Marriages Aren't Going Well...

You've heard a lot of the statistics—but they're worth repeating here.

In 1960, 1 out of every 50 people were divorced. Today, the number has risen to 1 out of 10.[1] The percentage of the population who are married has gone down from 72 percent in 1970 to 59 percent in 2002. Only 52 percent of marriages make it until their 15th anniversary, and only 20 percent of marriages make it for 35 years.[2]

---

1. http://www.census.gov/population/socdemo/hh-fam/cps2006/tabA1-all.xls.

2. http://www.divorcemag.com/statistics/statsUS.shtml accessed 2/13/2008.

These divorces have had dire consequences…

- ▮ We have become a fatherless nation. There are 72 million children in the United States of America eighteen years of age and younger. One-third of them will go to bed tonight in a home without a biological father.

- ▮ About 40 percent of busters, the generation born between 1965 and 1983, were raised by divorced or separated parents.

- ▮ James Dobson reports that 50 percent of the children born in a recent decade will spend at least part of their childhood in a single-parent home.[3]

- ▮ In one longitudinal study of twenty-five years, it was discovered that 40 percent of children from divorced homes never married, compared to 16 percent of children from intact families.[4]

- ▮ Children from divorced homes are also 40 percent more likely to get divorced themselves.[5]

- ▮ A child who grows up in a single-parent home is five times as likely to be incarcerated, to repeat a grade, and have emotional problems.[6]

What can we learn from these statistics? One thing's for sure—not resolving a crisis in your marriage leads to devastation. We are praying God might use this book to help you avoid those consequences. So if you're going through difficult days right now, we want to do several things in this chapter. We want you to identify what has made your marriage difficult, be convinced that your marriage is worth fighting for, and take some practical steps to make your marriage better.

---

3. J. Barbarino, *Children and Families in the Social Environment* (New York: Aldine de Gruyter, n.d.), 87, as cited in James Dobson, *Bringing Up Boys* (Wheaton, Ill.: 2001), 134.

4. Dobson, *Bringing Up Boys*, 64

5. National Center for Health Statistics, "Cohabitation, Marriage, Divorce, and Remarriage in the United States, Vital Health Statistics," ser.23, no. 23 (July 2002): 57; at www.cdc.gov/nchs/data/series/sr_23/sr23_022.pdf X

6. American Academy of Pediatrics, "Family pediatrics report of the task force on the family," *Pediatrics*, 111 (June 2003): 1541–71.

So What Makes a Marriage Difficult?

Marriage can be tough for a lot of reasons. You could have chronic financial trouble. You could be facing long-term health crises. You could have a child whose behavior and attitudes are tearing the house apart. You could have extended family members who cause stress and conflict at every turn.

But far and away the most common cause of a difficult marriage is a difficult spouse.

Pop Quiz!

Yes No

☐ ☐ Do you take pride that you let people know exactly where you stand on issues?

☐ ☐ Are you able to persuade other people to do things your way?

☐ ☐ Do you feel satisfaction when you get the last word in a conversation?

☐ ☐ Do you find it difficult to understand why it takes other people so long to figure out that your opinion is correct?

If you answer "yes" to any of these four questions, it's very possible that you are a difficult person to be with.

Types of Difficult People

Sue   Sue is a high-performance person. She really gets things done. Yet, in her rush to accomplish tasks, she regularly tramples on somebody's feelings. Her husband, Mark, often feels like he is walking on eggshells or trying to clean up the mess she leaves behind.

John   John is one of the nicest guys you'd ever want to know. For years he's been working on the next "big deal." The only problem is it's a pipe dream. The debts pile up, the bills are not paid, and John continues to live in his little fantasy world. Sarah tries to talk to him about it, and he doesn't get angry, he just spouts more positive thinking—"It's going to happen."

Tom   Tom is a great young man who also happens to be chronically unhappy with his life. Bitterness, resentment, and anger seethe just underneath the surface. At home, when he shuts the door and gets behind the closed blinds of his own private castle, he dumps all this out on his wife, Terri.

Kristin   Kristin is simply a negative person. She constantly finds fault with her husband, Tim. Nothing he does is ever good enough for her. The best Tim can do is pacify her so that she doesn't say anything.

Jeff   Jeff takes his lunch to work, so every day he makes a peanut butter and jelly sandwich. He lines everything up on the counter—the peanut butter, the jelly, his bread, and his Baggie. One day his wife was making a sandwich to take for lunch and she took her sandwich and put it in his Baggie. He exploded. "I can't believe you used my Baggie," Jeff said. "I had taken it out so I could put my sandwich in it." She was so mad, she took her wedding rings off and left them on the counter when she went to work.

Ginny   Ginny goes to church, is an incredibly capable businesswoman, and is also an alcoholic and addict. She's lost her license twice for driving under the influence. Her husband has seen her go in and out of rehab facilities for the past ten years. He's at the point where he doesn't care anymore—he just wants it to be over.

Well, they should. All marriages have hard times. But it's important to distinguish between "normal difficult" and "difficult difficult."

What's the difference between a normal person who is, from time to time, difficult and a difficult person who is from time to time normal? When does a normal person who's occasionally difficult become a difficult person? Here are two litmus tests. ***Is it*** *chronic?* and *Is it daily?* If you or your spouse are chronically difficult to get along with on a daily basis, then this is not normal behavior.

So what makes people difficult? Basically, people are needy, but some more than others. They have spiritual issues that have not been resolved, and they are emotionally immature. They are unhappy because they're primarily self-oriented. At some level, many of them feel like they have to take care of themselves because no one else will.

When you're married to a person who behaves this way for years and years, it can feel like it would be easier to quit and start over. Maybe you made an impulsive decision to marry this person. Perhaps looking back you realize you didn't use wisdom. You may have thought they would change and get better.

You also may have guilt from things you've done in the past and feel like you're being punished. "God, I don't deserve this. It's time to move on. I made a bad decision. I didn't think it through. Why should I have to be punished any longer?"

So the thought that "it would be so much easier to start over" gets compounded if you feel like you made a bad decision to begin with. And the world today is bombarding you with the message that if it doesn't work out, that's okay. There are very few social or cultural barriers to divorce anymore.

We understand how you feel. How can your marriage survive despite your circumstances? Our hope is that we can help you believe a truth so compelling that you would be willing to lay down your life for your spouse, even when they are chronically difficult to live with.

There's no magic formula we can give you to make your marriage wonderful. The only way through this is for you to get to the place where you can say, "I will lay down my life for my difficult spouse." What could help you say that? God's Word applied to your heart.

> Iwilllaydownmylifeformydifficultspouse is awfully long for a magic word…

This is especially hard when your spouse doesn't seem interested in helping things get better. Again, there are no easy answers. You have to be willing to lay down your life for your difficult spouse.

A (Slightly Disguised) True Story about…Difficult Days
Michael and Amy (continued)

Michael's dad worked all the time when he was little. When Michael hit his first home run in Little League, he looked to the stands searching for a dad who wasn't there. Michael made the decision he wanted to do it differently. He and Amy spend a lot of time with their children, and they provide them with whatever they need (and most of what they want), even when they can't afford it.

At one point Michael tried his hand at real estate, but he could never get over the hump. He even postponed a closing once to be at his son's baseball game, even though it would have been the only game he missed all season. Michael has also had trouble staying motivated as a leader at home. His dad certainly never modeled what a spiritual leader looked like—so Michael has been trying to figure it out from scratch.

Over the years, Amy has responded to the financial and relational stress by trying to control every aspect of her life. Like most married couples, during their early years they discussed almost everything. But now, twenty years later, Amy is making more and more unilateral decisions. She's lost respect for Michael because of what she sees as his indecision and apathy.

To be continued…

A difficult marriage can lead to a downward spiral.

The **Big** Idea

It is God's will for this marriage to work.

This big idea may not initially resonate with you. The natural thing in a difficult marriage is to try to figure out all the reasons why it won't work and how you can get out. But the Bible clearly says that it is God's will for your marriage to work.

You probably already believe this at some level—in theory. We want you to be a true believer; to know that this is **exactly** what God wants for your life and that it's also **exactly** what you want for your life. Only God's Spirit can do this in your heart.

Here are some passages to prayerfully consider:

> *"To the married I give this command, (not I but the Lord): A wife must not separate from her husband. But if she does, she must remain unmarried or else be reconciled to her husband. And a husband must not divorce his wife. To the rest I say this (I, not the Lord): If any brother has a wife who is not a believer and she is willing to live with him, he must not divorce her. And if a woman has a husband who is not a believer and he is willing to live with her, she must not divorce him.* (1 Corinthians 7:10–13)

It is God's will that this marriage work.

> *Then Peter came to Jesus and asked, "Lord, how many times shall I forgive my brother when he sins against me? Up to seven times?" Jesus answered, "I tell you, not seven times, but seventy-seven times."* (Matthew 18:21–22)

It is God's will that this marriage work.

> *"Haven't you read," he [Jesus] replied, "that at the beginning the Creator 'made them male and female,' and said, 'For this reason a man will leave his father and mother and be united to his wife, and the two will become one flesh'? So they are no longer two, but one. Therefore what God has joined together, let man not separate."* (Matthew 19:4–6)

It is God's will that this marriage work.

PLEASE DO TRY THIS AT HOME

Stop for a moment and pray. If you are not in a difficult marriage right now, pray for a friend who is. If your marriage is difficult, set aside the hurt, bitterness, discouragement, and doubt. Invite the Holy Spirit to change your heart. Pray that God would help you actually believe that you should lay down your life for your difficult spouse.

Finding Hope in the Midst of Difficult Days

How can you make it through another day if you feel stuck in a difficult marriage? We won't pretend that it's easy. Working with men for many years has shown us how complicated and painful some of these situations can be. But you really don't have any choice if you believe that it's God's will for your marriage to work.

Here are some ideas...

Look for Small Victories

The famous tower of Pisa is 187 feet tall, and constructed from marble. It began leaning shortly after construction started in 1174 and now leans fifteen feet at the top. Over the years, architects and scientists had tried various means of stabilizing the tower—many of which made it worse. In 1990, they shut the building down to tourists because the lean was becoming more and more pronounced. But in 1999, they finally tried something different. Every few days they removed about five gallons of dirt from underneath the high side of the building. That's only about one teaspoonful of dirt every minute under something that weighs 32,000,000 pounds. But in response, the building shifted a fraction of a centimeter. Over the next eighteen months, the lean of the building was reduced by sixteen inches, restoring it to what it was two hundred years ago. Scientists estimate this reduction will stabilize the building for at least the next three hundred years.

The scientists realized they couldn't undo nine hundred years of leaning in a few weeks. In the same way, you can't undo ten, twenty, or forty years of damage in your marriage overnight. Instead, look for small victories in your marriage.

Let's face it. You're almost certainly not going to completely change either you or your spouse. And you can't wait for your spouse to make the first move—that's a dead end. So what can you do together to stabilize your marriage for the next forty years?

What is one small, believable change YOU could make in your marriage? Is there even a teaspoonful of dirt that you could move to straighten your foundation? Find a good time and discuss this question with your spouse. Don't wait—take this step today.

For him: My teaspoonful of dirt to move is _____

_____

For her: My teaspoonful of dirt to move is _____

_____

No One Can Make You Unhappy without Your Permission

How do you engage with a difficult person without it constantly bringing you down?

"He who covers over an offense promotes love, but whoever repeats the matter separates close friends" (Proverbs 17:9). No one can make you unhappy without your permission. So, get in the habit of not giving your spouse permission to frustrate you. Cover over the offense. Don't talk about it with others or dwell on it.

"A man's wisdom gives him patience, it is to his glory to overlook an offense" (Proverbs 19:11). The New Living Translation says, "People with good sense restrain their anger; they earn esteem by overlooking wrongs." The Bible is a real-world book. This text doesn't ask you to pretend that sin doesn't exist. It tells you that you have the power to overlook an offense. The Holy Spirit can give you the wisdom and patience you need. No one can make you unhappy without your permission.

 Connection Point

> Think of a time when you interacted with your spouse recently and were able to make the situation better rather than worse. What was different about that experience? How can you duplicate that in the future?

---◆---

A (Slightly Disguised) True Story about… Difficult Days
Michael and Amy (continued)

About a year ago, Michael underwent major surgery that has required extensive rehabilitation. As a result, he's been out of work again. His inactivity during his recovery period has caused his weight to balloon. What was already a stressful situation in their marriage has now become a ticking time bomb. Michael doesn't enjoy talking about his situation because he's scared of what the future holds. Amy is frustrated because everything she says hurts Michael's feelings. She gets discouraged because he's not doing enough during his recovery to prepare for the future. She told us, "I feel hopeless when I look around and realize that nothing ever changes."

Fortunately, both Michael and Amy know Christ and are trying to follow Him. Amy has seen some small signs of growth. Michael's doctor has ordered daily therapy that is requiring him to be more active. And just the other day he volunteered to go to the grocery store during a football game to help Amy prepare for some guests. Amy is talking to a counselor, and they are both trying to be nicer and include each other. The lines of communication are opening up.

There are no quick fixes in sight—their finances are a mess, Michael has no real idea what his next job will be, and they certainly haven't turned into Mother Teresa and Billy Graham—but they still have their commitment that God can bring them through this together.

> Small steps that can change the direction of their marriage.

Imperfectly Happy or Perfectly Unhappy

Here's another really big idea: You must decide if you would rather be imperfectly happy or perfectly unhappy.

Happy people are happy because they learn to endure imperfect circumstances and find the joy in life. There are others who keep striving against what God has brought into their lives and end up perfectly unhappy.

If you think the first step of making it through a difficult marriage is to change your spouse, you are going to be perfectly unhappy. If you think the first step is to chuck it all and start over with someone else, you are going to be perfectly unhappy.

The first step is to really believe that God has called you to this marriage and He will give you the strength to make it through. It's not primarily about your happiness—it's about His glory. And He receives glory when you endure a difficult marriage with overlooking and grace-filled love.

In the quotation we included from Matthew (p. 43), Peter asked the question, "Lord, how many times must I forgive my brother? Up to seven times?" Jesus answered, "Not seven but seventy-seven times." We understand that it will be miserable at times if you have a spouse who requires this kind of forbearance. But Jesus says those who love His way do more than the "average" or "expected." You can make it through your difficult marriage if you follow Him. Your marriage will be imperfect—and may be difficult until the day you die—but it's better to be imperfectly happy rather than perfectly unhappy.

> **The worst situations can have glimpses of happiness. Take a moment right now and focus on one concrete thing about your spouse or marriage that brings satisfation, joy, or happiness.**
>
> **For him: I can be (imperfectly) happy because** _____
>
> _____.
>
> **For him: I can be (imperfectly) happy because** _____
>
> _____.

If you're in a difficult marriage, we hope and pray that some of what was said in this chapter can make a difference. Whatever else you do, don't give up hope. The gospel is God's power to change hearts—and He has changed men and women who had much harder hearts than your spouse. Will you choose to believe God and His Word over your feelings and desires? If you do, in the end you will experience His blessing. It truly is God's will for this marriage to work.

CHAPTER REVIEW

Have you been saying The Marriage Prayer every day? Fill in the blanks for the missing words. Give yourself 10 points for every blank you get correct.

For Him

Father,

I said, "'Til death do us part"—I want to _____ it.

Help me _____ _____ more than _____ ,

and her more than anyone or _____ else.

Help me bring her into Your _____ today.

Make us one, like You are _____ in _____ .

I want to _____ her, cherish her, and _____ her—

so she would _____ You more and we can bring You _____ .

Amen.

For Her

Father,

I said, "'Til death do us part"—I want to _____ it.

Help me _____ _____ more than _____ ,

and him more than _____ or anything else.

Help me bring him into Your _____ today.

Make us _____ , like You are three in one.

I want to _____ him, _____ him, and serve him—

so he would _____ You more and we can _____ You glory.

Amen.

You Haven't Finished this Chapter Until...

This is an incredibly important chapter. If you're in a difficult marriage, we've prayed that this could be a turning point. Take the time to listen— really listen—for God's voice.

So, don't go on to the next chapter until...

❑ You've done all the exercises, including the Please DO Try This at Home (p. 43) and The Connection Point (p. 45).

❑ You are making a habit of saying The Marriage Prayer every day.

❑ Together, you've talked through the reflection questions below and asked how these truths might apply to your life.

Questions for Reflection and Discussion

Use the questions to cement the ideas from this chapter into your marriage. Discuss them with your spouse and your small group of couples.

1. Think of a couple you know whose marriage is difficult. What is making it difficult.

2. What parts of "A True Story" in this chapter could you relate to? What aspects seemed foreign to you? What lessons could you learn from it for your marriage?

3. Does the big idea from this chapter resonate with you? Why do you think some couples have a hard time really believing that it is God's will for their marriage to work?

4. What is one practical take-away you gained from this chapter that you will implement in the next week? How will you do it?

A One-Hour Deposit for the Heart
Section 1: Faithfulness

You've started praying—"Father, I said, 'Til death do us part'—I want to mean it." Here's a deposit that can help you make that a reality.

Increase the security your spouse feels in your marriage by taking the time and effort to make special days—like your anniversary, Mother's Day, Father's Day, Valentine's Day, or a birthday—really special. So here's a handy guide to help you make an occasion something to remember. Use it on one of those days, or use it to make an ordinary day extraordinary. Make the commitment now that you both will use it at least once in the next year.

30 Days Before the Big Day...
☐ Start collecting thoughts for a letter you will write your spouse.
☐ If you want to invite others to participate in a dinner or celebration, prepare your invitation list.
☐ Order any online or catalog gifts or gift certificates.
☐ Ask your spouse for the date. Make it special: write a handwritten note, make a poster, hire a skywriter, get a banner made, a note in a bottle—use your imagination!

21 Days Before the Big Day...
☐ Make the dinner or brunch reservation at the restaurant, or plan the menu for your event at home.
☐ Invite guests so they have plenty of time to mark their calendars,
☐ Make progress on your notes for "The Letter."
☐ Other _____

14 Days Before the Big Day...
☐ Make sure your gift(s) have arrived; purchase or create a card.
☐ Other _____

7 Days Before the Big Day...
☐ Sit down with your accumulated notes and write "The Letter."
☐ Order flowers, a corsage, chocolate, gifts, or local gift certificates.
☐ Prepare homemade gift certificates (for chores, dinner out, night out w/ friends).
☐ Track responses to your invitations and connect with those you haven't heard from.
☐ Other _____

1 Day Before the Big Day...
☐ Have flowers or a gift—like a book—delivered "The Day Before" to prove forethought!
☐ Other _____

THE BIG DAY
☐ Start with breakfast in bed and a card for your spouse.
☐ Host the event. Make sure your spouse is able to enjoy themselves—NO WORK!
☐ Give your spouse "The Letter."
☐ Other _____

1 Day after the Big Day
☐ Write your spouse a handwritten note telling how much you enjoyed your date and why.

Section 2: Priorities

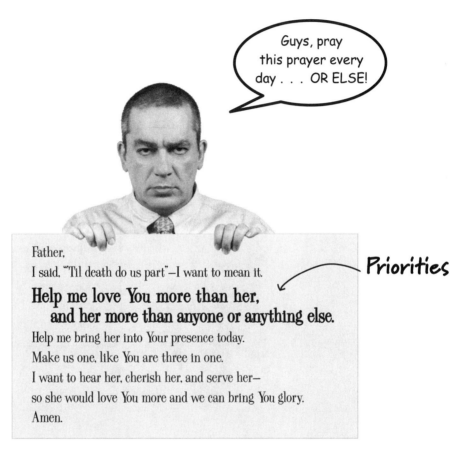

The next two chapters are about PRIORITIES. Priorities determine how we orient our lives. They are pre-decisions that shape the future we will bring to pass. In The Marriage Prayer, we're asking God to help us love Him first and our spouse second. If we keep this order, everything else in our marriage will fall into place.

In the next two chapters, we'll examine two big ideas:

> ▸ **We resolve conflict well when we exchange our natural self-focus for a God-and-spouse focus.**

> ▸ **Romance blooms when I cherish my spouse the way God cherishes me.**

Conflict and romance may seem like strange bedfellows for this section. But both of these areas reveal where we have placed our priorities.

We can't maintain the correct priorities in our own strength—that's why it's part of The Marriage Prayer. Begin each day asking God to shape your priorities: "Help me love You more than her, and her more than anyone or anything else."

Are you sure you can afford to read this section? Don't you know what time it is? You have e-mails to answer, places to go, phone calls to return, kids' homework to check, shopping to do...

3: Conflict

Fighting for Your Spouse's Heart

Okay, let's get started with another quick question. Go with your first thought. (Don't spend any more time thinking than you spend brushing your teeth.)

What would you say are the greatest sources of conflict in your marriage?

Him:

- ❏ Money
- ❏ Stress
- ❏ Children/parenting
- ❏ Neglect

- ❏ Sex
- ❏ In-laws/extended families
- ❏ Hobbies / Interests
- ❏ Other _____

- ❏ Communication
- ❏ Work
- ❏ Friends

Her:

- ❏ Money
- ❏ Stress
- ❏ Children/parenting
- ❏ Neglect

- ❏ Sex
- ❏ In-laws/extended families
- ❏ Hobbies / Interests
- ❏ Other _____

- ❏ Communication
- ❏ Work
- ❏ Friends

How well would you say you deal with conflict in your marriage? Check all that apply...

- ❏ We have open communication and deal thoroughly with conflict right away.
- ❏ We talk about the surface sources of conflict but are unable to talk about the root issues.
- ❏ We love each other, so it's just easier to ignore conflict and pretend it didn't happen.
- ❏ We really don't have much conflict to deal with.
- ❏ There is so much conflict I just get emotionally tired of trying to deal with it.
- ❏ I've learned to avoid conflict by letting my spouse have their way most of the time.
- ❏ Other _____

RULES OF ENGAGEMENT

Take no more than five minutes to talk about your answers with your spouse (we want to keep things moving).

What surprises you? Why?

A (Slightly Disguised) True Story about…Conflict
Jim and Cindy

When was the last time you felt that way?

Since it was getting close to Christmas, Jim had decided to take a few days off, mainly to work on a major project around the house. He woke up early, answered a few e-mails on the computer, and prepared to take the car to the shop for routine service. When he woke Cindy to ask her to meet him at the mechanic's, he could sense her agitation. When they got home from the auto shop, Cindy wanted to make a special breakfast of waffles for the family. Jim had already planned a busy day, but knew they should make time for the breakfast. He was trying to squeeze in a shopping trip with the two youngest children for their mom; their oldest had gotten sick the night before and couldn't go. Their daughter had a lunch outing planned with friends. They also had guests coming over that night for dinner, and the inside of the house looked like you would imagine at the end of a very busy week. Cindy felt overwhelmed. By the time she finished making waffles, she was so frustrated with how the day was shaping up that her head was hotter than the waffle iron. They had schedules to keep, so Jim ran out the door with the kids.

To be continued…

Even though the gospel is true, we still have to manage against the reality of the fall. Things will never be exactly the way they should be in a broken world. So while you may hope Jesus is going to make all your marriage problems miraculously disappear, the reality is you will always have disagreements and conflicts. (They should lessen over time, but they will never fully go away, even if they eventually become mild disagreements [like who moved the false teeth].)

However, if you begin to pray and believe The Marriage Prayer, you will want to love God more than your spouse, and your spouse more than anyone or anything else. Doing it any other way eventually ends in frustration and tears. Conflict comes when something else begins to take first or second place in your heart.

Each conflict either ends up driving you apart or drawing you together—there is no middle ground. Conflict hurts, but in God's hand conflict becomes an opportunity to realign our priorities. We can stop, reevaluate, and have our hearts reshaped by the power of what Jesus does for us in His death and resurrection. When God changes our perspective, conflict becomes a chance to fight for our spouse's heart.

The Big Idea

We resolve conflict well when we exchange our natural self-focus for a God-and-spouse focus.

Where Conflict Comes From

Before we can resolve conflict and allow it to help us grow, we need to know where it comes from. So what are the sources of conflict in a marriage? The two main sources of conflict are *priority* problems and *moral* problems.

The biggest of all priority problems is neglect. It's too easy for us to take each other for granted and forget about the emotional bank account that we talked about in chapter one—taking more withdrawals than we are making deposits.

When Daniel and Angela started dating, they talked all the time. They shared their hopes, dreams, ambitions, and fears. They talked about everything—how many children they wanted to have, places they wanted to visit, things they wanted to do. They were inseparable.

Then they got married and began to build a home. Emotionally, Angela stayed connected to Daniel and their future family; but Daniel went off to work the day after the honeymoon and basically forgot to come home. He conquered her, and now went off to conquer his next big challenge.

One day, about a month later, Angela confronts her husband.

Angela: "I thought we were going to build a life together."

Daniel: "We are, sweetheart. But first I have to put a few
            deals in place. I need to hit this hard so we can get
            ahead. Then I'll be back; you can count on me."

Angela loves Daniel and trusts him. So she decides to stay where she said she would be. But a week becomes a month, a month becomes a year, which becomes two. Again she confronts him.

Angela: "Daniel, you're working a lot. Why'd we get married
            if we're never going to see each other?"

Daniel: "I know it's been a rough couple of years, but I'm about
            to become the youngest regional director in the history
            of the company. If I get this promotion we'll be set."

She cares for him. She wants to believe him. Time goes on and little Jesse comes along. Then Taylor. Two years becomes five, five becomes ten.

One day Angela's running the kids to school and can't catch Daniel on the phone because he's in a meeting. It hits her.

Every day the idea grows. When she's convinced it's true, she slowly begins to drift away emotionally from where she said she was going to be.

Daniel's very bright and feels the difference right away, so he rushes back to where he said he would be in their marriage vows. He begs and pleads with Angela to come back. No matter what he says, though, she just keeps drifting away. Nothing he can say will bring her back. What Daniel doesn't understand is that Angela is emotionally dead, and he killed her through neglect.

Unfortunately, we hear this story all too often. A few years ago, David saw this played out in the life of a neighbor. Matt came over one night in tears—Amy had asked him to leave. The money quote from the conversation? "I've been doing whatever I wanted on weekends for the last ten years and now she just doesn't love me anymore."

Seven great tips for creating conflict—all in one place!

Thoroughly Field-tested Tips on How to Drive Your Spouse Away

Learned from personal, empirical, and practical experience

No. 1—Work. Try to make your spouse understand how hard you are working. You're tired and grumpy because of all the work you are doing for the family.

No. 2—Stress. Ask your spouse to be more understanding about the pressure you are under. In fact, say, "Honey, you have no idea how much stress I'm under." This goes over big with a spouse under their own stress.

No. 3—Logic. Explain all the reasons why your spouse's feelings are wrong. "Look at all these different reasons that you've arrived at an illogical conclusion."

No. 4—Punctuality. Heave a big sigh the next time your spouse gets in the car three minutes late to head to church.

No. 5—Fix Them. "You know, if you would just lose about twenty pounds you'd be so much happier."

No. 6—Pout. Go over in your mind all the wrongs your spouse has done to you and let the depth of your grievance show on your face. That'll get him!

No. 7—Keep Score. Track all the ways your spouse has let you down. Act like you forgave and forgot, but harbor the details until you need them.

PLEASE DO TRY THIS AT HOME

Which of these six tried-and-true methods hit home with you? Is there another that immediately comes to mind? Discuss with your spouse the one you believe YOU are most guilty of, and then ask their opinion.

Why Conflict in Marriage Hurts So Much

Since we truly have become one flesh, there is a vulnerability in marriage unlike any other relationship. Whether we admit it or not, we care deeply what our spouse thinks about us. We desperately want to be admired, cherished, respected, and valued. When we experience conflict and criticism, it strikes directly at this desire—we are forced to admit our failings and faults.

Not only this, but most of us are considerably more sensitive than we want to let on. When we get our feelings hurt at work or by a friend, we have to control ourselves so we don't let it show. We look like we have crocodile skin. But the reality is that often we are faking it. Those things that people say to us matter. Rejections, slights, and rude comments really do hurt.

We really are a lot more sensitive than we would ever admit.

Most of us tend to bring 100 percent of our sensitivity into 20 percent of our relationships. These are the relationships where we feel comfortable expressing our frustration or hurt feelings. We accumulate all the little pent-up slights we get all day, perceived or real. Since we won't honestly deal with the people who caused the issues, we bring 100 percent of our sensitivity home with us. So the slights or criticisms we experience at home get blown all out of proportion. The next time you react to something your spouse says, take a deep breath and consider what all might lie beneath your emotional reaction.

◆

A (Slightly Disguised) True Story about…Conflict
Jim and Cindy (continued)

Besides his regular stressful job, Jim was also working on a few things at church, and a major project around the house. Cindy had three kids to deal with—two teenagers—as well as her own responsibilities at church and with friends.

They'd been getting by for a few weeks heading toward Christmas, including a five-day visit by the in-laws, but finally the stress of it all got the best of them.

Cindy began treating Jim as if he could do nothing right, and Jim did his best to avoid Cindy and find time to finish his project.

It's the season for giving… STRESS!

Jim and Cindy had one last errand to run before Christmas, and they wanted to do it together. They drove to the music store to pick out a keyboard for their children. On the way to the store, Cindy

told Jim he was being irrational with some of the demands he was placing on the kids, like asking their youngest to be in bed by 9:30 last night. It was Christmas vacation. At first Jim was defensive. In the moment, he was tempted to say that if there was more discipline in the house then he wouldn't have to step in— but he was smart enough to keep his mouth shut. When they got to the store at 9:20, the parking lot was empty. That's because the store didn't open until 10:00.

So Jim and Cindy sat in the car. In the empty parking lot. Barely speaking. It was going to be a long forty minutes.

To be continued…

Conflict from Immoral Choices

Another source of conflict in marriage is moral failings. Often, spouses make sinful decisions in the area of sexuality, money, relationships, substance abuse, and time. When these things come to light, the pain and betrayal often leads to intense conflict.

Some people reading this book are in the middle of trying to restore a marriage broken by the sinful choice of their spouse. It can feel hopeless and desperate when you are in the moment. You feel violated, used, unloved, and abandoned. Nobody likes to feel that way—hence the conflict.

Do you know the irony of these tragic and devastating situations? We do.

For example, a female friend is in a marriage where her husband had an affair with their college-aged baby sitter. The young woman attended the same church as their family. What a gross and disgusting betrayal, on so many levels. After the events, his wife decided to stick with the marriage and try to make it work. A number of years later, a long way into his repentance, she said this, "If I had to go through what we went through to have the marriage I have now, I would do it all again. I never want to go back to the superficial marriage we had before."

They don't have to, and neither do you. Many couples who've been through devastating failures tell us that their marriages are now better than ever before. That can be your story too.

 **Connection Point**

> Can you think of a difficult experience you have been through that has helped your marriage? What did you learn?

Resolving Conflict

One essential thing we've found from experience: if you want to have great relationships, honest communication has to be at the foundation of it all.

Too often in relationships there is a lack of frankness. Often we decide what to say based on what we think the other person wants to hear. We try to say everything so carefully because we are trying to manage the other person's response.

Don't get us wrong. We should be sensitive and thoughtful in the way we speak to our spouses. But many of us cross a line where we are not expressing the whole truth because we are afraid of how our spouse will react. When this becomes a habit, you have no real way of dealing with conflict.

Learn to speak the truth in love and let God determine the results. Speak with gentleness, humility, and a genuine desire for the other's person's best interest.

One practical way to foster honest communication: Don't focus on your spouse's behavior; instead express how you are impacted as a result of their behavior.

You also foster honest communication when you think ahead and don't have to reinvent how to handle conflict every time it occurs. Make an actual plan for how you will bring up and handle conflicts. Here are a few suggestions (mark beside each one that you actually want to try to implement):

Want to do it?

Him   Her

❑   ❑   Set up a time once a week when you can bring up any issues outside the heat of the moment. Have the meeting whether or not there are any issues to discuss, so the habit will be in place when there is a problem.

❏ ❏ You might want to raise an issue by writing down your perceptions and feelings—make that part of the system. It's easier to say what you mean when you take the time to write it down. Then give your spouse a few minutes to read the letter and think about their response before you have your conversation.

❏ ❏ As soon as a conflict begins, go to a specific place in your home to discuss things calmly and privately. Your friends and children don't need to see you sounding off at one another in a public setting. (Your kids will know something is up, so it's a good thing to loop back with them and explain the conflict and your resolution. They need to see you own up to mistakes and also to see that your love for one another is bigger than any temporary issue.)

❏ ❏ Make the commitment together now: The next time conflict begins, take time out from one another to slow the adrenaline. You may want to each pray The Marriage Prayer to reorient your thoughts. Then come back together to talk about resolving the issues.

NBAS (No-Brainer Action Step)

Talk with your spouse about the suggestion you'd like to do.

The secret of functional families is honest, open communication, especially when it comes to conflict resolution. Remember, nobody can make you unhappy unless you give them permission. Having honest communication is one way of denying permission to someone else to make you unhappy.

A (Slightly Disguised) True Story about…Conflict
Jim and Cindy (continued)

After a few minutes sitting and thinking in the parking lot, Jim has had a chance to pray and reflect on what was really going on in his heart. He realizes his behavior with the kids was a response to how he felt—he was losing control in the home and needed to intervene to restore order. He confesses this to Cindy, then he tells her he should have talked with her before making his "pronouncements." In response she confesses that she had been allowing the stress in their life to make her pull away from him.

Jim and Cindy could have treated these events as if they were just about one particular day. But because they are willing to communicate honestly about core issues, they begin to deal with his desire for control and her negativity.

The value of open and honest communication.

Finishing their errands moves from a miserable experience to a positive one as they connect emotionally. They know the conflict may not be totally finished, but they also know it will no longer keep them apart. By talking things through, they show they are willing to fight for each other's heart.

Long-Term Conflict

These are two great questions. It's frustrating when your spouse promises, promises, promises, then lets you down. How do you deal with that?

We find the relevant principle for this situation in Matthew 6:14–15. It says, "If you forgive men when they sin against you, your heavenly Father will also forgive you." Watch this—"But if you do not forgive men their sins, your Father will not forgive your sins." Notice that this text does not say, "If someone will apologize for their wrongdoing then you must forgive their sins." It says, "You must forgive them their sins."

We realize this is not easy, but the principle here is that you should count the cost of withholding forgiveness from someone even when they don't deserve it. Over time, unforgiveness destroys relationships. If you hold anything against anyone, forgive him so that your Father, in heaven, may forgive you your sins.

A good friend allowed himself to be drawn down a bad path over a period of years and ended up visiting a prostitute. Shortly after that, his wife found some things on his computer, and the truth came out. Friends in the church rallied around them, and he repented, but she still had a choice to make: Would she try to make the marriage work or not? Because this had gone on at various levels for so long, she knew this might not be the end of the story. Would she forgive him and walk with him through his addictive issues and their consequences?

> *A Note of Caution...*
>
> **We aren't talking about abuse...** Conflict is very different than abuse. If you are in a relationship that includes physical abuse, verbal abuse, debilitating addictions, or abandonment —please get professional help. Take steps to immediately protect yourself and any children involved.

She chose to stick it out and fight for her husband's heart. She moved beyond her natural self-focus. God has blessed her choice by giving her back a grateful and loving husband and father.

Remember our big idea: **We resolve conflict well when we exchange our natural self-focus for a God-and-spouse focus.** When we make our spouse our top priority (after God), we will still have conflict, but now we have a full emotional bank account and the reserves to handle conflict well. This is why we are praying every day in the Marriage Prayer—"Lord, help me love You more than him, and him more than anyone or anything else."

CHAPTER REVIEW

Match the missing word(s) on the right with the key idea on the left.

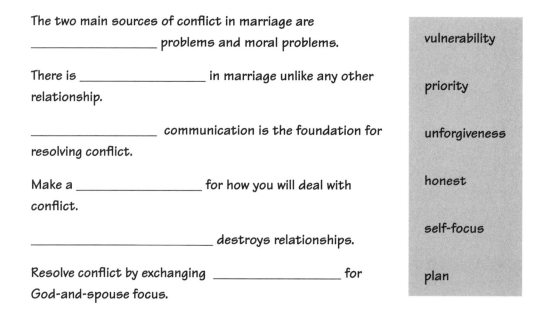

The two main sources of conflict in marriage are
_____ problems and moral problems.

vulnerability

There is _____ in marriage unlike any other
relationship.

priority

_____ communication is the foundation for
resolving conflict.

unforgiveness

Make a _____ for how you will deal with
conflict.

honest

_____ destroys relationships.

self-focus

Resolve conflict by exchanging _____ for
God-and-spouse focus.

plan

You Haven't Finished this Chapter Until. . .

A lot of hard-earned lessons went into this chapter. We prayerfully expect that God will use it to help you deal with conflict in your marriage. But that's only going to happen if you actually allow Him to change your mind and heart!

> **So, don't go on to the next chapter until...**
>
> ❑ You've done all the exercises, including the Please Do Try This at Home on p. 58 and the No-Brainer Action Step on p. 63.
>
> ❑ You are praying The Marriage Prayer every day.
>
> ❑ You've talked through the reflection questions below with your spouse and asked how these truths might apply to your life.

Questions for Reflection and Discussion

Use the questions to cement the ideas from this chapter into your marriage. Discuss them with your spouse and your small group of couples.

1. Why do you think conflict is so emotionally charged in a marriage? What are some factors that make it difficult for you to deal with conflict?

2. What parts of the "A True Story" in this chapter could you relate to? What aspects seemed foreign to you? What lessons could you learn from it for your marriage?

3. Does the big lidea from this chapter resonate with you? How can you cultivate a "God and others" focus in your life?

4. What is one practical take-away you garnered from this chapter that you will implement in the next week? How will you do it?

4: Romance

Cherishing Your Spouse's Heart

We're going to start things off with a quick exercise. When you hear the word "romance," what comes to mind? Check all that apply...

Him

- [ ] time
- [ ] touching
- [ ] travel
- [ ] closeness
- [ ] sex
- [ ] food
- [ ] effort
- [ ] conversation
- [ ] adventure
- [ ] Other _____
- [ ] Other _____

Her

- [ ] closeness
- [ ] food
- [ ] effort
- [ ] candles
- [ ] conversation
- [ ] time
- [ ] gifts/flowers
- [ ] touching
- [ ] sex
- [ ] Other _____
- [ ] Other _____

RULES OF ENGAGEMENT

Sit down with your spouse and take a few minutes to discuss the words you chose. What insights did you gain from listening to your spouse's choices?

A (Slightly Disguised) True Story about...Romance
Kevin and Laura

Kevin finished placing his few groceries on the conveyor belt and waited for the woman in front of him to finish paying. After she put her receipt in her purse and pushed her cart away, Kevin stepped up to the cash register.

Curtis, the checkout clerk, looked up with a smile. "Hey, Mr. Sanders. Light load today. Where's Mrs. Sanders?"

"She's at home—I just ran in to pick up a few things."

As Kevin left the store holding his two plastic bags, he couldn't help but smile at what had just occurred.

Kevin and Laura had come a long way in the last ten years. Theirs was an all too familiar story—married twenty-two years at the time, kids just left the house for college, he'd been working and traveling too much for years, she had been so focused on the children that she ignored him. They didn't spend time together, and they'd allowed themselves to drift apart.

One telling day, Kevin gave Laura grief for reading so many romance novels. Her response, "Reading these books is the only way I can get any romance in my life."

To be continued...

Ouch! Has there been a time your spouse could have said something like that?

Romance is the "**IT**" of marriage. When IT is there, wow! You know what IT is like. IT is how you felt the first time you kissed your spouse. IT was what you felt when you took that long walk in the moonlight. IT is the smile she gave you when you surprised her on her birthday. IT makes all the difference—the sun shines brighter, the birds sing more beautifully, the skies are bluer, every word is a melody, and every touch an electric thrill.

But when IT is gone, watch out. Every task becomes drudgery, every conversation endless, every joke annoying, and every muttered remark a personal slight.

IT is pretty important, but can also be fleeting. So what is romance anyway, where does it come from, and how can we keep it alive for the long term?

What Is Romance Anyway?

Romance: n. (rō-´man(t)s) A mysterious or fascinating quality or appeal, as of something adventurous, heroic, or strangely beautiful.

Romance and sex are not the same thing. Sex is important—we give it a whole chapter later in the book. But while sex is an activity within marriage, romance is an atmosphere that can characterize your marriage.

None of us feel romantic all the time. Romance is only produced under "special circumstances." Researchers have been doing a lot of work to understand what this looks like in the human brain. They've recently identified three different areas that light up during romantic encounters.[1] These three areas work together to connect momentary romantic feelings to the memory of the particular person who is helping to create them. God has wired our brains to translate feelings of romance into a long-term relationship!

How does this cycle in our brain get kick-started? There are many biological explanations for the thrill of romance—including scent, hormonal levels, etc.—but the underlying reality is that a romantic encounter occurs because we connect with another person at the level of our spirits. They know us, they like us; we know them, we like them—sparks fly.

Romantic feelings come easy for two twenty-three-year-olds celebrating their engagement, but how do we continue to experience romance in the long-term commitment of marriage?

The **Big** Idea

Romance blooms when we cherish our spouse the way God cherishes us.

In Christ, each one of us is intimately known and accepted by God. He loves us more than we could ever imagine, and He cares for us meticulously on a moment-by-moment basis. He is always looking out for our good. Because we were created by God to receive His love, we long to be cherished like this. When we experience God's love through His Spirit, we know that it is deep and real and right.

Your spouse is a person who knows they were made to be loved with this kind of love. So we create romance in our marriage when we cherish our spouse by treating them with consideration, courtesy, and respect. That's why we are praying in The Marriage Prayer, "Help me love You more than her [him], and her [him] more than anyone else." Giving our spouse the top priority shows we hold them in the highest regard.

---

1. Scientists have learned that (1) the brain's ventral tegmental supplies dopamine, (2) the nucleus accumbens interprets "thrill signals" from other regions of the brain, and (3) the caudate nuclei store patterns and mundane habits. The first area signals this event is something special, the second interprets those signals and links them to the current circumstances, and the third area establishes a connection to the memory of the actual person who created these feelings. Jeffrey Kluger, "Why We Love", *Time,* January 28, 2008, 58–59.

Romance in the Bible

The Bible is not silent in the area of romance. It gives us the example of Jacob and Rachel (Genesis 29). Jacob worked seven years for Rachel, but her father gave him Leah instead. Jacob then worked seven more years for Rachel. (Now that's romantic!) Jacob showed incredible regard for Rachel, and cherished her until the day he died.

The Bible also contains one of the most romantic poems in the history of literature. In the Song of Songs, the lovers are virtually overcome with their passion for one another. They experience a borderline fixation...

> *How beautiful you are, my darling!*
> *Oh, how beautiful!*
> *Your eyes behind your veil are doves.*
> *Your hair is like a flock of goats*
> *descending from Mount Gilead.*

Guys—probably not a good line to use today.

> *Your teeth are like a flock of sheep just shorn,*
> *coming up from the washing.*
> *Each has its twin;*
> *not one of them is alone.*

> *Your lips are like a scarlet ribbon;*
> *your mouth is lovely.*
> *Your temples behind your veil*
> *are like the halves of a pomegranate.*
> (4:1–3)

> *My lover is radiant and ruddy,*
> *outstanding among ten thousand.*

> *His head is purest gold;*
> *his hair is wavy*
> *and black as a raven.*

> *His eyes are like doves*
> *by the water streams,*
> *washed in milk,*
> *mounted like jewels.*

His cheeks are like beds of spice
    yielding perfume.
His lips are like lilies
    dripping with myrrh.

(5:10–13)

We'd suggest reading the whole book. While it's difficult in some places for us today to understand the narrative, it's easy to understand the imagery. This bride and groom were deeply in love and romantic to the core.

Where Romance Comes From

Some mornings when you go outside, there is dew all over the ground, almost like after a heavy rain. Other days the grass may be nearly dry. Why the difference?

Dew forms out of the air when the temperature drops low enough to cause the moisture in the atmosphere to condense. The more water vapor in the air, the higher the temperature at which dew forms. The dryer the air, the colder it has to get.

Romance in a marriage is like dew condensing from the air. If the atmosphere of your marriage is dry, romance is hard to come by. Rather than being romantic, small actions toward one another—a smile, a word, a held hand—can seem forced or even manipulative.

But if you saturate your marriage with love, time, and affection, then small moments of connection mean a lot more than an outsider might think. In the right conditions, those small, tender actions condense into something that becomes romance.

How can you help your spouse feel cherished? It won't usually come as a by-product of a few big actions; it will flow out of the atmosphere from lots of little things that demonstrate daily love.

A (Slightly Disguised) True Story about…Romance
Kevin and Laura (continued)

After the kids had left home, Kevin and Laura sat down one Saturday morning to talk about getting a divorce. For years they'd been complacent—just letting their marriage go wherever it wanted. And it had. Slowly but surely it had gone downhill. Now they wondered if it had gone past the place of no return.

She was tired of being lonely and angry, and he was tired of taking grief at home on top of his already stressful life. She felt ignored and betrayed. He wondered where the excitement and fun had gone. They both were fed up.

They discussed what they considered to be their two options—get a divorce and put themselves out of their misery, or build a real marriage and make it work. They talked about the pain and anger that they felt toward each other. They walked through the steps that led them to this point, and what they could do about it. After a long discussion, Kevin and Laura decided to rebuild their marriage.

As they held hands at the end of their discussion, they knew it wouldn't be easy to undo the damage that had been done.

To be continued…

They made the decision to start cherishing each other again.

When Romance Is Gone

In our busy world, it's easy for the feeling of romance to fade away. "There's just no fire there." "He doesn't love me anymore." "She acts like I'm her brother, not her lover." "It feels like we're just living together as roommates."

We hear comments like this from men and women all the time. What's going on when this happens? There are at least two possibilities.

You might have unrealistic expectations. Every day won't feel as electric as what you experienced in the movie theater as a twenty-year-old. The loss of jobs, sick in-laws, teenagers whose grades aren't what they should be, the death of a friend, and intense projects at work—life is not a chick-flick. Life is filled with all kinds of circumstances that simply cannot be romantic. That's okay.

As Pat has said before, all disappointment is a result of unmet expectations. Make sure you and your spouse are on the same page about the stresses and realities of what's happening in your life right now. Your life-stage and current circumstances profoundly affect the state of your romantic relationship.

Still, if weeks and weeks go by with no romance, then there's a problem. Often what has happened is that we have forgotten to treat our spouse with care and respect. We've misplaced our priorities and let other things distract us from moment-by-moment care for your spouse.

Why is there a lack of romance in your marriage? Perhaps you've forgotten what your "love" actually looks like to your spouse. You aren't actually cherishing your spouse the way God cherishes you. You don't love God more than them and them more than anyone or anything else. When we "love" like this, romance withers and dies.

First Corinthians chapter 13 is a great diagnostic to evaluate our daily love. It shows us how true love acts toward others. Perhaps you've read it many times, but what if we made this passage specific for you? How would your love measure up?

Insert your name in the blanks below (where "love" appears in the original).

_____ is patient, _____ is kind. _____ does not envy, _____ does not boast, _____ is not proud. _____ is not rude, _____ is not self-seeking, _____ is not easily angered, _____ keeps no record of wrongs. _____ does not delight in evil, _____ rejoices with the truth. _____ always protects, _____ always trusts, _____ always hopes, _____ always perseveres.

 **CONNECTION POINT**

Which quality on the previous page do you feel you do best? Are there several that show your love is falling short? Say a brief prayer asking God to change your heart, then share your answers with your spouse.

I've got some things to work on. How should I go about it?

Glad you asked. Here are some key ideas for how to create an atmosphere that promotes romance. As you read them, consider which one might best apply to your situation.

■ **Talk about special memories.** Reconnect by remembering your first date, the night you became engaged, or important moments in your early marriage. It's too easy to forget all that God did to bring you together.

■ **Have lots of little interactions with your spouse.** A whirlwind getaway to a New York City luxury hotel won't be romantic when disconnected from the hundreds of interactions from the previous weeks. Hold hands, ask an open-ended question, send a text greeting to her cell phone, fold clothes together, call from the car on the way home, or fix your spouse a surprise bowl of ice cream. Take advantage of the little opportunities life presents.

■ **Spend time together.** Make a point to spend some time together each day for the next week or so—take a walk, play a game, or do the dishes. Before you go to bed, make sure you've done something together that included quality time.

- **Buy a gift for each other.** Set a reasonable dollar limit and both go shopping to buy a small gift for one another. Plan a quiet evening and give your gifts along with the reason you selected it.

- **Make sure your spouse knows that you think they're great.** Nothing is more romantic than knowing that someone really likes you. Every person wants to be highly thought of. Find one good thing about your spouse and mention your appreciation every day. Or find a special time, look your spouse in the eyes and mention three things about him or her that you think are wonderful.

- **Write a letter, by hand.** Here's a corollary to the previous idea: Put down on paper some of things you are grateful for about your spouse. Choose a special moment to present the letter to him or her; make sure your spouse has peace and quiet to enjoy your note.

- **Ask questions every day.** Don't let the pace of life rob you of a chance to share your thoughts, ideas, and dreams…and to hear theirs. Keeping communication and intimacy alive is a prerequisite for romance. Talk with your spouse about things they are interested in. Ask nonthreatening questions that show you care.

 ## NBAS (No-Brainer Action Step)

Choose one of the ideas above to do right away. Don't tell your spouse which one you picked—yet. Begin to implement your choice, then come back in a week or so and talk about any changes you've noticed in your relationship.

The Link between Sex and Romance

Romance connects the emotional and the physical. Typically, a woman needs to feel a romantic connection emotionally so she can love a man physically. And typically a man needs to feel a romantic connection physically so that he can love his wife emotionally.

So both of you have to compromise. This is why Paul says, "Husbands ought to love their wives as they love their own bodies." Show your spouse the same regard that God shows for you.

Author Gary Chapman has a wonderful insight in his book *The Five Love Languages*.[2] We tend to love our spouses the way **we** want to be loved, not the way **they** want to be loved. For example, the best deposit Pat Morley's wife, Patsy, would enjoy in her emotional bank account is an act of service. So for a long time in their marriage she was always doing things for Pat. Meanwhile, the best deposit Patsy could make for Pat would be to spend quality time with him. So he was trying to do anything he could to spend time with Patsy.

They were loving each other the way they wanted to be loved, not the way the other person wanted to be loved!

It's natural for us to think that our spouses appreciate the same things we do. But if you want to love your spouse like your own body, you have to understand how they want to be loved, and love them that way.

PLEASE DO TRY THIS AT HOME

How does your spouse want to be loved? How about you? Which of these would you appreciate the most?

❏ acts of service   ❏ receiving gifts   ❏ quality time

❏ physical touch   ❏ encouragement   ❏ other _____

Share your answer with your spouse. Does anything surprise you about their response?

---

2. Gary Chapman, *The Five Love Languages* (Chicago: Northfield, 2004).

◆

A (Slightly Disguised) True Story about…Romance
Kevin and Laura (continued)

To make their marriage work, Kevin knew he had to change. He rearranged some things about his business life so he could be home more. He and Laura began to intentionally spend time together and include one another in their lives.

Kevin hadn't been in a grocery store in fifteen years, but now he made the commitment to shop together. That's how they'd gotten to know Curtis.

Kevin learned that the kitchen wasn't just a place to store the refrigerator—he could actually cook and clean with Laura. They played cards and board games together. They learned how to talk to one another again. When he traveled for work, Laura took a few days vacation and came along.

After they recommitted to building their marriage, they planned a long vacation trip several months in advance. They had a garage sale to help finance the trip. They sold items on eBay. They researched where to stay and what to do. After the trip, they realized they had as much fun planning the trip together as they did actually taking it. God had restored their marriage.

And Laura hasn't picked up a romance novel in years.

They had learned to cherish each other again.

Every marriage needs romance. No one wants to go through life with a spouse who is more like a business partner or a roommate; we all go into marriage looking for a lifelong lover and companion. Take steps this week to enhance or reignite romance in your marriage. Show the same regard for your spouse that God shows for you. And continue to pray, "Help me love You more than her, and her more than anyone or anything else."

CHAPTER REVIEW

An anagram is the rearrangement of the letters in one word to spell another word or words. Like "evil" and "vile." Or, better for this book, "marriage" and "garner air." Unscramble the important words from this chapter. We've completed the first one for you. (If anagrams and puzzles are not your thing, feel free to look at the answer key on page 215.)

Anagram		Key Word from Chapter
intact expose	=	expectations
core man	=	_____
rich she	=	_____
rented	=	_____
nice con not	=	_____
spectre	=	_____

You Haven't Finished This Chapter Until...

Romance is a vital part of any marriage. If you've found your heart growing cold toward your spouse, let this be an opportunity for God to speak to your heart.

So, don't go on to the next chapter until...

❑ You've done all the exercises, including the Connection Point (p. 77), and Please DO Try This at Home (p. 79).

❑ You've made praying The Marriage Prayer every day a habit.

❑ Together, you've discussed the reflection questions on the next page.

Questions for Reflection and Discussion

Use these questions to cement the ideas from this chapter into your marriage. Discuss them first with your spouse and then with your small group of couples.

1. How would you rate the level of romance in your marriage on a scale from 1 to 10? Is it better or worse right now than in the past? Why?

2. Did the "A True Story" in this chapter remind you of anything you have experienced? What lessons can you apply to your marriage?

3. How do you define "cherish"? What does that look like to you? Guys, how would you put that in your own words?

4. What is one practical action step each of you can do? What will that look like?

A One-Hour Deposit for the Heart

Section 2: Priorities

How can your prayer—"Help me love You more than her (him), and her (him) more than anyone or anything else"—become a reality? One great way to make your spouse a priority is to spend time with them and communicate. Plan an evening when you will have an hour or so alone. Using two markers (such as a dime and nickel), take turns rolling a die* and moving your marker. Follow the instructions wherever you land on The Priorities Board Game.

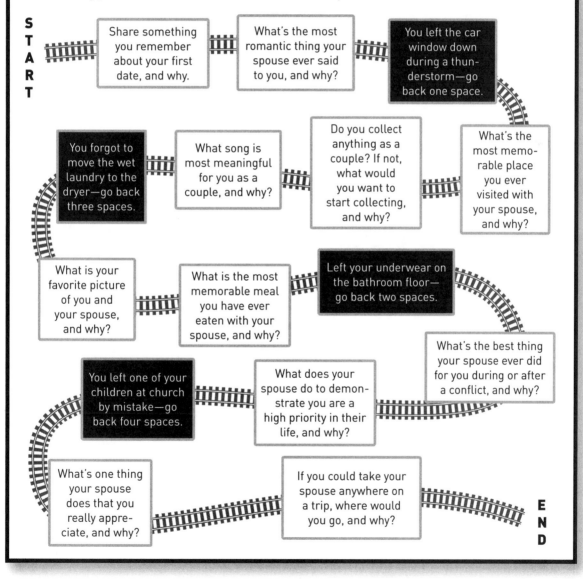

S T A R T

Share something you remember about your first date, and why.

What's the most romantic thing your spouse ever said to you, and why?

You left the car window down during a thunderstorm—go back one space.

You forgot to move the wet laundry to the dryer—go back three spaces.

What song is most meaningful for you as a couple, and why?

Do you collect anything as a couple? If not, what would you want to start collecting, and why?

What's the most memorable place you ever visited with your spouse, and why?

What is your favorite picture of you and your spouse, and why?

What is the most memorable meal you have ever eaten with your spouse, and why?

Left your underwear on the bathroom floor—go back two spaces.

What's the best thing your spouse ever did for you during or after a conflict, and why?

You left one of your children at church by mistake—go back four spaces.

What does your spouse do to demonstrate you are a high priority in their life, and why?

What's one thing your spouse does that you really appreciate, and why?

If you could take your spouse anywhere on a trip, where would you go, and why?

E N D

*If a die is not available, use the digits from your social security number in consecutive order, skipping any that are larger than six.

Section 3: Purpose

Guys, are you saying The Marriage Prayer every day?

Father,

I said, "'Til death do us part"—I want to mean it.

Help me love You more than her,

and her more than anyone or anything else.

Help me bring her into Your presence today. ← Purpose

Make us one, like You are three-in-one.

I want to hear her, cherish her, and serve her—

so she would love You more and we can bring You glory.

Amen.

The next two chapters are about PURPOSE. There's a reason God ordained marriage. He gives you a job to do with your spouse. In one sense it's not a hard job—because it's what He made you for.

In another sense it's very difficult, because it's so easy to go on autopilot and let your marriage drift.

If you don't remember your purpose, your marriage will lack direction.

In the next two chapters, we'll examine two big ideas:

▶ **Our marriage will thrive when we both submit to God's divine order.**

▶ **Marriage works well when we worship well.**

Life is filled with challenges that can distract us from our true purpose. We need constant reminders to help us stay on track. And we need the power of the Holy Spirit working in our hearts every day.

That's why we pray as part of **The Marriage Prayer**, "Help me bring her into Your presence today."

5: Roles

Serving Your Spouse to Help Them Flourish

All of us have different roles we have been required to play. Some we did well; some brought pain and frustration. Place a ✓ beside the role below that seemed to fit you best. Then place an X beside one that brought stress, embarrassment, or shame.

Him:
- ❏ Student
- ❏ Peacemaker
- ❏ Class clown
- ❏ Son
- ❏ Rebel
- ❏ Victim
- ❏ Athlete
- ❏ Geek
- ❏ Hero
- ❏ Friend
- ❏ Stud
- ❏ Other _____

Her:
- ❏ Student
- ❏ Peacemaker
- ❏ Class clown
- ❏ Daughter
- ❏ Rebel
- ❏ Victim
- ❏ Athlete
- ❏ Geek
- ❏ Hero
- ❏ Friend
- ❏ Hottie
- ❏ Other _____

RULES OF ENGAGEMENT

Take a break and sit down with your spouse. Consider the role where you placed your check. Why did you select that as the one that fit you best? Looking at where you placed an X, why was that role more of a struggle?

◆━━━━━━━━━━━◆━━━━━━━━━━━

A (Slightly Disguised) True Story about... Roles
Eric and Kelly

Kelly looked from the paper to the man behind the counter. "Let me try my husband one more time." Turning away, she hit redial on her cell phone for the fourth time. After six rings, she heard the familiar sound—"You've reached Eric's phone—leave a message." She snapped the phone shut. She took a deep breath, then faced the man. Picking up the pen, she signed the bottom of the sheet. "If it really needs it, I guess let's just do everything you recommend."

Have you ever had a day like this?

↘

Today had been one of those days that brought everything to a head. Not only was Eric out of town again, but the kids had to be at three places at once. His mom had called and bulldozed her emotionally about seeing the kids more. Now the car had broken down. She'd been trying to reach Eric most of the day, and he still wouldn't answer his phone. So here she was, talking to a mechanic about something she knew nothing about. And she had to handle it all on her own. The day felt like a perfect example of everything wrong with her life.

To be continued...

───────────────────────────

Here it comes. This is the chapter some of you have been waiting for. A few of you will write us letters. (We'll read every one.) Others of you may write us off and won't even bother. (We hope not—give us a chance. ☺)

This chapter is important because it's about authority—and that's one subject our culture is really confused about. Because our culture is so confused, a lot of the men and women we talk to have trouble figuring out what to do.

What does the Bible really say about the roles of a husband and a wife? This chapter might be the most controversial in this book, but it could also be the most helpful. If you disagree with what we have to say, pray about it. Find something in the chapter that has merit and act on it—then see if it rings true.

A Dramatic True-Life Episode Demonstrating Disregard for Authority...

The Scene: Pat's house, specifically, his driveway.

The Background: Over the years, Pat's been able to tell stories about the neighborhood kids on bicycles who use his driveway as a cut-through between the two streets on either side of his house.

The Immediate Circumstance: Pat was walking out in the morning to get the newspaper when he looked up and saw a guy in a red Jeep coming down his (Pat's) driveway. Our scene opens with Pat walking over to the guy's (a.k.a. Jeep Man) window...

Jeep Man: I guess I'm busted, huh?

Pat: (with a smile) You sure are. What are you doing?

Jeep Man: Well, I live over there, and we just bought a second house on the other street that I'm fixing up. I thought I would cut through here to get to the new house.

Pat: You realize this is a private drive, right?

Jeep Man: (hesitating) Actually, I didn't know for sure.

Pat: Come on, give me a break here. This is a concrete driveway and there are shrubs all around. It's a very residential look. And the front of my house is no more than fifteen feet from the driveway. Doesn't it give the general impression that this is a private drive?

Jeep Man: (with resignation) I'll give you that.

Pat quickly told him the story about the kids who always cut through his driveway. Pat said, "People complain about this generation of kids, but if you and I would have a little respect for authority, they might also."

Anything but Authority

Authority is out of vogue today. No one likes to obey rules and regulations; we all want to go our own way.

Yet all authorities are in place because God put them there (Romans 13:1). Without respect for authority, there would be chaos. There is a natural order to the world, and things only work right when people live within that natural order.

For example, what if people just ignored the police?

What would happen if the moon said to the earth, "I think I'll just go my own way today?" There would be chaos in the solar system.

What if Jesus had said to the Father, "Sorry, no cross for me, Dad!" We would all still be suffering spiritual chaos from the guilt of our sin.

In the same way, we have chaos in our culture because people renounce submission to God's divine order. And this is most obvious when it comes to our families.

What the Bible Says

We'd like you to read the following Scriptures. We are including so many for a reason—
we really want you to see how consistent and thoroughly the Bible treats this subject:

Submit to one another out of reverence for Christ.

*Wives, submit to your husbands as to the Lord. For the husband is the
head of the wife as Christ is the head of the church, his body, of which he is the
Savior. Now as the church submits to Christ, so also wives should submit to
their husbands in everything.*

*Husbands, love your wives, just as Christ loved the church and gave
himself up for her to make her holy, cleansing her by the washing with water
through the word, and to present her to himself as a radiant church, without
stain or wrinkle or any other blemish, but holy and blameless. In this same
way, husbands ought to love their wives as their own bodies. He who loves
his wife loves himself. After all, no one ever hated his own body, but he feeds
and cares for it, just as Christ does the church—for we are members of his
body. "For this reason a man will leave his father and mother and be united
to his wife, and the two will become one flesh." This is a profound mystery—
but I am talking about Christ and the church. However, each one of you also
must love his wife as he loves himself, and the wife must respect her husband.*
(Ephesians 5:21–33)

*Wives, in the same way be submissive to your husbands so that, if any of them
do not believe the word, they may be won over without words by the behavior
of their wives when they see the purity and reverence of your lives . . . Husbands,
in the same way be considerate as you live with your wives, and treat them
with respect as the weaker partner and as heirs with you of the gracious gift of
life, so that nothing will hinder your prayers.* (1 Peter 3:1–2, 7)

The first task
of a man is to
love his wife.

The first task
of a woman is
to respect her
husband.

A husband
should be
considerate.

Husband and wife are inter-dependent, not independent.

Now I want you to realize that the head of every man is Christ, and the head of the woman is man, and the head of Christ is God... In the Lord, however, woman is not independent of man, nor is man independent of woman. (1 Corinthians 11:3, 11)

A woman should learn in quietness and full submission. (1 Timothy 2:11)

He must manage his own family well and see that his children obey him with proper respect... A deacon must be the husband of but one wife and must manage his children and his household well. (1 Timothy 3:4, 12)

Likewise, teach the older women to be reverent in the way they live, not to be slanderers or addicted to much wine, but to teach what is good. Then they can train the younger women to love their husbands and children, to be self-controlled and pure, to be busy at home, to be kind, and to be subject to their husbands, so that no one will malign the word of God. (Titus 2:3–5)

A husband loves his wife, but a wife should also love her husband.

That's a lot of information, and it takes time to digest and discuss the details. But at this point, is there really any doubt or ambiguity about the major themes in the Bible when it comes to husbands and wives?

We're not naïve; we know some people reading this book won't like this. It sounds out-of-date in our modern world. But, despite how some modern scholars have tried to twist the Bible, it's really intellectually dishonest to say, "It's ambiguous. God has not made His position clear."

We are Bible teachers, not culture teachers. Our prayer is that all Christians would **revere God's Word** and **transform the culture**. But because the culture and the Bible are so different, there's a lot of pressure to **revere the culture** and **transform God's Word**. We won't do that—no matter what anyone thinks.

When the culture and the Bible are walking in parallel, it's easy to live as a Christian. But when the culture pushes one way and the Bible teaches something else—there's pressure. Then well-meaning people come up with all sorts of explanations of what the Bible teaches on these subjects. But the Bible itself remains clear.

What These Scriptures Teach

Ed Cole, the late "grandfather of the Christian Men's Movement," used to tell a humorous story about a man who learned for the first time at a seminar about his role in the family. He was so excited; he went home and told his wife, "I'm supposed to be the head of this household." Then for thirty minutes he repeated everything he'd heard, everything she was doing wrong, and how he was going to set things right. After that, he didn't see his wife for about a week.

Then, after about six days, he could see her just a little bit…out of his left eye.

So what are a few things we can learn from the previous texts?

I see at least two major things:

One, the husband is the "head" of his wife, so he needs to be a servant leader.

Two, the first task of a husband is to love his wife, and he needs to do it like Christ loved the church.

I agree. But I also see that:

While we submit to one another, the wife has a special calling to submit to her husband.

And…

A wife should respect her husband and allow him to lead, and he should treat his wife with consideration and respect.

That's right. The Bible teaches **mutual love** and **mutual submission**.

- ▌ The husband loves his wife by actively living as a servant leader.

- ▌ The wife loves her husband by submitting to him and treating him with respect.

- ▌ The husband submits to his wife by living under the authority of Christ and treating her as a "fellow heir of the gracious gift of life" (1 Peter 3:7).

- ▌ The wife submits to her husband by allowing him to lead the household.

At the most basic level, what the Bible teaches is that there is a divine order to creation. One of the biggest keys to a thriving marriage is mutual submission. But submission to what? **Submission to the divine order of creation.**

It's not primarily about me. It's not even primarily about us. It's about getting our relationship aligned with God's divine order.

The **Big** Idea

Our marriage will thrive when we both submit to God's divine order.

◆

A (Slightly Disguised) True Story about... Roles
Eric and Kelly (continued)

For a few years, Kelly had been taking responsibility for more and more things in her marriage. She planned the vacations, she handled the money, and she made decisions about the kids' education. When Eric did step up, she got frustrated because he didn't care enough or do things as well as she wanted him to. It was simpler to do it herself.

For Eric, Kelly's desire to control was one part of a long process that led to him disengaging. Kelly was intense and emotionally unpredictable, so it was easier for Eric to withdraw than connect. He began to look at his occasional trips for work as a chance to get away. Sometimes Kelly cried when he left. After a while that just made him angry. What does she think I can do about it? It's not like I'm gone every week.

Eric felt like he'd tried early on to be a leader. But he and Kelly's issues and backgrounds made it difficult for him to know what that actually looked like.

Kelly had been abused by an uncle as a young girl and hadn't yet come to terms with how destructive that really was. Eric's dad hadn't been a great role model—he reacted to Eric's mom's strong personality by letting her do whatever she wanted to do. Over several years, Eric found himself following in his dad's footsteps.

Then Kelly found the pictures on their home computer.

To be continued . . .

Living under Authority

There is a divine order to Creation and a divine order to families. There is a husband, there is a wife, and there may be children. When everyone submits to their proper role, marriages and families thrive.

Why is this so controversial? One reason it's controversial is that our culture says that for something to be fair it has to be exactly the same. This is a fallacy. How should we define "fair" biblically? **"Fair" is that each person gets an opportunity to use all their gifts, talents, and abilities to bring the maximum glory to God.**

Ironically, when we pursue an absolute equality in roles we are actually being unfair—because men and women no longer can live the way God designed them to live.

Yet many men today feel pressure to be more like women, and many women feel pressure to be more like men.

Ted tries to be so sensitive and submissive that he refuses to lead—it's painful for others to watch him flounder. Mary asserts her independence by trying to control everything—especially her husband. She's hard to be around because she wants to dominate every situation. Ted and Mary are living out a corruption of the other gender's role.

Many young adults basically think men and women are the same except for a few differences in their body parts.

When men and women are confused about their roles, chaos reigns. You may have served on a committee before where you had two people both trying to run it. That's called a power struggle. When you have two people trying to run a marriage, neither of whom is in mutual submission to God's created order, then you're going to have power struggles and chaos.

Not long after Pat and Patsy got married, she started coming up with statements like, "You can't tell me what to do" and "I need to reach my full potential." So Pat finally had a frank discussion with her and asked, "Where is all this coming from? You weren't talking like this six months ago." After some discussion, they realized that as a young woman she was being influenced by secular women's magazines. Their marriage was not conforming to God's divine order, and it began to create chaos.

At other times, Pat had not treated Patsy with respect and affection, and he'd thrown the marriage into chaos. But they've been able to sort it out because they have learned that the key to a thriving marriage is mutual submission to God's created order.

God really meant what He said—there is a divine order of Creation. When there is not respect and submission to this divine order, then there can't be lasting peace and joy in your relationship. In the stress and confusion of our modern world, we need an army of couples faithfully applying God's Word to our culture.

Glad you asked.

Part of what marriage is all about is helping your spouse become everything God wants them to be. That's why Paul says a husband should love his wife like Christ loves the church, "to present her to himself as a radiant church, without stain or wrinkle or any other blemish, but holy and blameless" (Ephesians 5:27).

When you live the role in your marriage that God intended, it is an act of service that God uses to bless and grow your spouse.

It's also the only way that you can become everything God wants you to be. Ironically, as long as you are shirking your role, or usurping your spouse's, you can't fully blossom. You'll always be stunted and deformed by trying to live your own way rather than in alignment with God's created order.

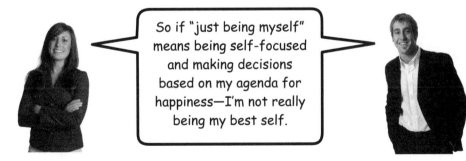

That's right, you're actually being a diminished version of who God wants you to be—a spiritual "Mini-me." The real way to "be yourself" is to do what God has called you to do in your marriage, allow Him to transform your heart, and actively serve your spouse.

How do you realign a marriage with God's divine order of Creation?

You and your spouse need to talk through your respective roles and agree on what God is calling you to do. Husband, take responsibility to be a servant leader. Wife, God is calling you to love and respect your husband.

Rate yourself on the following scale:

How well are you living out the role that God intended for you in your marriage?

Him: ■——————————————————————————————■
        Poor   Excellent

Her: ■——————————————————————————————■
        Poor   Excellent

Take three minutes and discuss why you rated yourself the way you did. Do you agree with where your spouse rated themselves? Why or why not?

What are some steps to get back to your correct role?

For a man, save some of your time, energy, creativity, and passion and invest it in your family. You can't use it all up at work. Don't allow your wife to step up and carry the whole load. Be engaged with the family finances, be involved with the kids, help out with decisions about the house and yard. You can't be a servant leader unless you show that you are willing to invest your heart and soul into your marriage. This is what your wife is looking for.

Too many men today are shirking. If you're not loving and leading, no wonder your wife is stepping up. Stop being the weaker partner. Be involved as a strong, contributing partner. That's what you are. The Bible says that, and everybody knows it—even if nobody in our culture wants to admit it. TV sitcoms may cultivate the stereotype of the man who is a buffoon. Step up and be a godly man.

For a woman, this means you need to step back and allow your husband to step up. Submission is not a sign of weakness, and it does not mean being a doormat—it means living in right relationship to God's divine order. You still need to work together and come to mutual agreement, but allow your husband to take the lead. If you over-function and take care of all the tasks in your marriage, you are enabling him to under-function and become passive.

God has built the husband to be the warrior for the family. If a wife decides to step in front, she can fight for a long time. Eventually, though, she will get beat up. She's not equipped with the armor. Even if your husband is not doing a great job—he still has the armor and calling from God. Stay behind him where you are protected.

Besides, as someone has said, submitting just means ducking so that God can hit your husband.

A (Slightly Disguised) True Story about…Roles
Eric and Kelly (continued)

After his original denials, Eric came clean—he'd been dabbling in things off and on for years, and even been with a woman he met online. Kelly was devastated. It took a while, but through the help of guys in his small group and counseling, Eric came face-to-face with his sin and the addictions it spawned. He repented and reached out to restore his broken relationship with Kelly. Over time, he found that the reason he was acting out sexually wasn't about sex at all. He tried to allow God to meet his deepest needs and started investing in his marriage. Even though he didn't know exactly what it looked like, he renewed his commitment to be a servant leader.

As Kelly tried to pick up the pieces, God gave her the grace to see that it wasn't just about Eric's sin. She began processing her own brokenness and failures. She realized that her controlling and nagging was more about her than Eric. Her emotional outbursts came from her own insecurity—she refused to trust Christ, Eric, or anyone else. For too long, she'd usurped Eric's authority because being in control was more important than trusting God.

After counseling, she became persuaded to risk it and let Eric be the leader. This felt really scary but she soon realized that living out the role God had for her—as Eric's wife—was the safest place to be.

Eric and Kelly still struggle—this isn't the kind of thing just goes away in a few months or even a few years. But they have found that even in the tough times, their marriage works when they live in submission to God's created order.

Defining Roles in Your Marriage

All couples have to determine how to apply biblical principles to a modern marriage. What roles do your spouse and you have in your marriage?

Use the following chart to discover the roles of each of you play. Put an X on the side of the chart for the person who has primary responsibility for each aspect of your marriage. If the other person has partial responsibility, put a check on their side. If it's shared equally, put an X on both.

Him		Her
	Earning income	
	Managing finances	
	Household chores—dishes, laundry, etc.	
	Outdoor chores—lawn, trees	
	Car maintenance	
	Discipline of children	
	Education/homework with children	
	Spiritual growth of children	
	Major household purchases	
	Vacation planning	
	Family schedule	
	Other:	
	Other:	
	Other:	

Connection Point

Based on your answers, do you have a "workable" division of labor in your marriage? Do you think this is the way God wants you to be doing it? If not, what changes should you make.

A Checkup

Here's a very practical way to move forward. Do a checkup to see if something or someone is taking you away from *your key role*. For the husband, that's being a servant-leader. For the wife, that's being one who respects his leadership. For both, that means serving the needs of the other.

Jerry got a checkup the hard way. He wanted to give a testimony in front of a men's group, so he asked his wife, "Who's #1 in my life?" She said, "Work."

"What?" Jerry asked.

"Work is #1 in your life."

"No baby, you're #1 in my life."

She stared at him. "I am not #1 in your life, and the only person you're kidding is yourself."

Is something taking you away from your role in your marriage? Is there a hobby, friendship, activity, book, game, career, or interest that is keeping you from serving your spouse? Are you pulling away because you don't want to deal with conflict? Is it easier to just stay in the same old roles than return to biblical standards? Is there an area of your marriage where the two of you disagree—such as how to handle your teenager—and you are not submitting to each other? If any of these things are true, you're violating God's order of Creation.

Connection Point

How did you answer the questions in the last paragraph? What is one thing that is likely to distract you from fulfilling your role well? Talk about that briefly with your spouse.

Remember the big idea from the very first chapter: After God, but before all others, make your spouse your top priority.

The greatest, most profound relationship in God's order of Creation is husband and wife. This is the key to a thriving marriage—mutual submission to God's created order. When we live out our role, we can fulfill God's purpose for our marriage. That's why we pray, "Help me to bring him into your presence today."

CHAPTER REVIEW

Find the following hidden words (see the answer key on page 215 if you need help):

ROLES	AUTHORITY	RESPECT	LOVE	SERVANT
HEAD	SUBMISSION	ORDER	DIVINE	FAIR
DISTRACTION	CREATION	CONSIDERATE		

```
E  F  C  R  R  M  M  A  D  Z  R
L  F  A  S  E  R  V  A  N  T  D
G  O  F  I  D  S  E  L  O  R  I
Y  D  V  E  R  H  P  F  P  E  V
E  A  T  E  O  C  R  E  S  T  I
N  O  I  T  A  E  R  C  C  E  N
C  O  N  S  I  D  E  R  A  T  E
N  O  I  T  C  A  R  T  S  I  D
N  O  I  S  S  I  M  B  U  S  F
L  S  Y  T  I  R  O  H  T  U  A
E  D  R  I  T  E  O  I  S  E  A
```

You Haven't Finished This Chapter Until...

Getting your roles straight is foundational to having a great marriage. This could be a chapter that God uses to take your marriage to the next level. Don't shortchange yourself or your spouse by not really listening to what God might be trying to say.

So, don't go on to the next chapter until...

- ❑ You've done all the exercises, including the Connection Points (p. 101, 102).

- ❑ The Marriage Prayer has become a part of your daily routine.

- ❑ Together, you've discussed the reflection questions on the next page and talked about how these truths might apply to your life.

Questions for Reflection and Discussion

Use the questions to cement the ideas from this chapter into your marriage. Discuss them with your spouse and your small group of couples.

1. Has our culture's confused view of roles in marriage affected you? How? What has God used to help you see more clearly?

2. What parts of "A True Story" in this chapter could you connect with the most? What aspects were most different from your experience? How can you apply what you read to your marriage?

3. Does the big idea from this chapter resonate with you? Why or why not? Why is it hard to live under authority? What makes it particularly difficult when it comes to marriage?

4. What is one practical take-away you garnered from this chapter that you will implement in the next week? How will you do it?

6: Worship

Living with Your Spouse in the Presence of God

Here's an exercise to get you started. Remember, this is meant to be quick. Go with your first answer.

When do you feel most connected to God?

Him

- ☐ Looking at God's creation
- ☐ Helping someone
- ☐ Exercising
- ☐ In the mountains
- ☐ When I'm close to my wife
- ☐ At church
- ☐ With my kids
- ☐ At night
- ☐ In the morning
- ☐ Other _____
- ☐ Reading the Bible
- ☐ With friends
- ☐ At the beach

Her

- ☐ Looking at God's creation
- ☐ Helping someone
- ☐ Exercising
- ☐ In the mountains
- ☐ When I'm close to my husband
- ☐ At church
- ☐ With my kids
- ☐ At night
- ☐ In the morning
- ☐ Other _____
- ☐ Reading the Bible
- ☐ With friends
- ☐ At the beach

RULES OF ENGAGEMENT

Spend a few minutes talking with your spouse. Why did you pick the answer you did?

A (Slightly Disguised) True Story about… Worship
John and Michelle

As they hung up the phone, John and Michelle felt they were at the end of their rope. They turned out the light in their bedroom, held each other, and cried.

As a new stepmom, Michelle was trying to be as supportive as she could for John. John's children were having a tough time, and their oldest was in full-blown rebellion. They had just spent over an hour on the phone with an old friend who was an expert with adolescents. They listened as he shared his experiences and talked through their choices. None of their options seemed particularly good. Now as they lay in the darkness, they cried out to God asking how they got to this point and what He wanted them to do.

This was John's second marriage and Michelle's first. John's children hadn't handled it well when their mom left. And things weren't getting much better with Michelle in the picture.

The behavior of their oldest child was becoming reckless and dangerous—so much so that it was time for some tough decisions. Now, if they could just figure out what the right choice was.

To be continued…

Can you identify with how they felt?

No way am I sitting around all day singing hymns with my wife. Why a whole chapter on worship?

We understand worship may seem like a strange topic for a marriage book. But hey, the book's been okay so far, right? So trust us a little.

What is worship?

We devoted this chapter to worship so we could explode some misconceptions about it and also show how central it should be to our lives. We'll also discuss why it's so important to your marriage. By the end of the chapter, we hope it will be even more meaningful when you pray, "Help me bring him (or her) into Your presence today."

One classic definition of worship is "the direct acknowledgment to God of His nature, attributes, ways and claims, whether by the outgoing of the heart in praise and thanksgiving or **by deeds done in such acknowledgment.**"[1]

We realize that's a lot of words, so feel free to read it again. The first half of that definition is standard—that's what we normally think of when we think of worship. The last phrase reveals a part of worship that we might not normally consider.

Yes, we worship when we sing songs in church, pray, or read our Bible. But we also worship whenever we live out of a heart of faith in God.

At every moment when we acknowledge God's presence and priority, we are worshiping—whether we are washing dishes, changing a diaper, closing a sale, driving a car, or hearing a sermon. All of life is worship.

Okay. I'm assuming you're going to flesh that out. But if all of life is worship, then what does it mean to not worship?

---

1. W.E. Vine, *Expository Dictionary of New Testament Words*, p. 236, emphasis ours.

We're glad you asked. **We stop worshiping when anything becomes more important than God.**

You see, there's a sense in which worship is the central fact of human existence. God made us to worship Him. And we're pretty sure that if it's the central fact of human existence it must be important to your marriage!

The Battle for Your Heart

A fierce battle rages for the hearts and minds of people. It's not new—from the beginning in the garden of Eden, God required that Adam and Eve worship Him. They chose not to.

It's the same today. God reaches out for us, but we ignore Him and worship idols of our own design. And our marriages suffer the consequences.

History is the story of this battle. When God rescued the Israelites from Egypt, He called them to worship Him alone (Exodus 20:1-4). They chose not to. Then He sent judges to call the people back to Himself. Instead, they "did as [they] saw fit" (Judges 17:6; 21:25). Then He gave them kings to lead them into proper worship. Instead, they did evil in the sight of the Lord and set up altars to false gods on the high places (1 Kings 14:22–24). Then He gave them prophets to call the people to repentance. But they did not listen (Jeremiah 5:4–5).

Then Jesus came and won our hearts back for God. When we were dead spiritually, He made us alive again. And He made us alive so that we could love the Lord our God with all our heart, soul, mind, and strength (see Mark 12:30).

With a new heart and the presence of the Holy Spirit, we have power to acknowledge God's presence and hand in every part of our lives. We can worship in all of life because of what Christ has done for us.

Worship requires that we have reverence for God. Our culture tries to trivialize God and cut Him down to a manageable size. But in the Bible, when people see and know the mighty God they fall on their face in awe (for example, see 1 Kings 18:38–39). One sign that you are worshiping well is that your view of God has gotten bigger. Worship puts God back where He belongs as the Lord of the universe.

The Big Idea

Marriage works well when we worship well.

Why is worship important in marriage?

Let's see: God made it the first commandment (Exodus 20:3), then Jesus reiterated it as the most important thing. That probably means worship matters in marriage.

Worship is the foundation that keeps the rest of your life on track. When we take our focus away from Christ and start looking to something else, we begin to be deceived about every area of our life.

Without her glasses, David's wife, Ruthie, would be legally blind. She wears contact lenses during the day, but when she removes those contacts at night she can't see anything. Everything is a blur. She walks through the house like a zombie—hands out in front of her trying to avoid bumping into anything and falling.

True worship is like eyeglasses for the soul. **It allows us to see the world for what it really is.** When our hearts are aligned with God, we can make sound judgments about values, priorities, desires, needs, etc. When we take our eyes off Christ and look at something else, everything becomes hazy and blurry. What used to be so clear is now not so cut and dried. This is how we get off track—our hearts and minds begin to focus on something other than God. Once we stop seeing the world correctly, we begin to justify all our other actions.

Every sin flows out of a lack of worship of God. You can't pursue an inappropriate relationship outside your marriage while you are worshiping God. You can't ignore your family by working too much or pursuing a hobby while worshiping God. You can't emotionally disconnect from your spouse while truly worshiping God.

Not only that, but **worship also puts all the rest of life in perspective**. When we lose our focus on God, our problems and circumstances look really big.

But when we worship, we are reminded how big God is, and our problems are put back in perspective.

Worship changes the calculus of our perspective quite a bit. God is not sitting in heaven wringing His hands about how all this will work out!

Don't take worship lightly. Everyone who gets serious about living all of life before God will have a revolution in their heart and mind.

Since we live in a world that doesn't worship, people who do worship are going to stand out. Friends will wonder why you give thousands of dollars to your church and other ministries. Neighbors will wonder why you use your vacation to go on mission trips. People will think you're crazy for not buying a replacement for your eight-year-old car and giving the savings for the new building. If you haven't done anything recently that some people would think was stupid, you may not be worshiping.

PLEASE DO TRY THIS AT HOME

Have you done something for God in the last few years that might seem extravagant to people who don't know Christ? How does that reflect what you worship?

A (Slightly Disguised) True Story about… Worship
John and Michelle (continued)

John and Michelle were both Christians when they met. They had an active ministry together through their church, and enjoyed spending time with other couples. As they went through the tough time with their kids, they were grateful for all that God was teaching them through the gospel. They never felt like He loved them any less. They never doubted that He had their best interests at heart. They learned that if He received glory any circumstance was worth it.

Sure, they got tired of the struggle and had their down moments.

And it wasn't always obvious what to do, so they got in the habit of inviting other Christians into their lives for wisdom and support. They learned to keep short accounts with each other and communicate well, because they knew they had to be on the same page. They spent time reading the Bible personally, praying together one-on-one, and attending Bible study groups through their church.

So when their oldest child become a reckless rebel, God protected them from an attitude of bitterness; instead He gave them an attitude of trying to learn how they could grow. They both knew that God often uses hard times to shape us to be the people He wants us to be.

They understood how worship put their problems in perspective.

To be continued…

How to Win the Daily Battle for Your Marriage

We win the daily battle for our marriage by winning the daily battle over who or what we will worship. Here are some ideas to help you stay on track each day.

Live each moment in light of the presence and lordship of God. Brother Lawrence was a monk who lived in the 1600s. His short treatise, *Practicing the Presence of God*, explains how his life changed when he began actively including God in every aspect of his day.

> I worshipped Him the oftenest that I could, keeping my mind in His holy Presence, and recalling it as often as I found it wandered from Him. I found no small pain in this exercise, and yet I continued it, notwithstanding all the difficulties that occurred, without troubling or disquieting myself when my mind had wandered involuntarily. I made this my business, as much all the day long as at the appointed times of prayer; for at all times, every hour, every minute, even in the height of my business, I drove away from my mind everything that was capable of interrupting my thought of GOD.[2]

> Pray remember what I have recommended to you, which is, to think often on GOD, by day, by night, in your business, and even in your diversions. He is always near you and with you; leave Him not alone. You would think it rude to leave a friend alone, who came to visit you: why then must GOD be neglected? Do not then forget Him, but think on Him often, adore Him continually, live and die with Him; this is the glorious employment of a Christian; in a word, this is our profession, if we do not know it we must learn it.[3]

What Brother Lawrence learned was that we were made to acknowledge God in every moment of our lives. He's the king of the universe. He demands and deserves our undivided allegiance.

---

2. http://www.ccel.org/ccel/lawrence/practice.iv.i.html.

3. http://www.ccel.org/ccel/lawrence/practice.iv.x.html.

It doesn't matter how mundane the activity—God has called you to it and wants to be a part of it. Every time our thoughts return to God, the Holy Spirit has a chance to renew our minds and perspective. We can once again see the world the way it truly is.

NBAS (No-Brainer Action Step)

Think of something you do every day, like brushing your teeth or starting the car. Got it in mind? Now before you do that task tomorrow, stop and say a thirty-second prayer to acknowledge God. Pray something like, "Father, today is Your day. Help me remember that You are with me every minute of the day. I don't want to live out of my strength—I need the strength and wisdom of Christ. Let me live for Your glory."

Preach the gospel to yourself every day. That may sound like a funny phrase. You probably don't consider yourself a preacher. We could have written, "Beat it into your stubborn head that Jesus really does love and forgive you. And do it until you really, really believe it." But that's kind of harsh and hard to remember. So we'll stick with "Preach the gospel to yourself every day."

Each of us needs to remember that we are cherished children of God. He made us, and if we have asked for forgiveness then He has forgiven us and adopted us as His own. There is nothing we can do to earn more love from Him.

You don't have to prove yourself to anyone. You don't have to be good enough. You don't have to impress. You don't have to make people need you or say you are okay.

So often it's not our sin that keeps us from God, but our self-righteousness. We think we are doing good enough, so we stop throwing ourselves on the mercy and grace of God. Moralism is the philosophy that says that my religious performance makes me a good enough person to please God. When we're honest, most of us would have to admit that we suffer from it at times.

Moralism kills true worship. If I'm good enough, then why do I need to worship God? The gospel says that we are not good in ourselves; we are forgiven and made righteous through faith in Christ. God loves it when His children rely completely on Him.

The God of the universe loves you and will never let you go. When we believe that deep in our souls, we are free to be who He has called us to be.

NBAS (No-Brainer Action Step)

If you have a child, sing the song "Jesus Loves Me" with them now. If not, and you're alone, sing it anyway. (But if you're with other people, especially strangers, perhaps you should just sing it in your mind.)

Pray with your spouse. We did a Google search on the words "spouse pray together." 1,390,000 Web pages were returned in the results. So the idea that you should pray with your spouse is not exactly new. But based on our informal research, those search results probably contained about 25,000 Web pages each for every couple that actually prays together. (The only thing that is talked about more and actually done less may be reading the Bible.)

This point is not very complicated. God wants us to **pray...with...our spouse**. So rather than belabor it, we're going to ask you to stop right now and actually do it.

NBAS (No-Brainer Action Step)

Take a moment and pray with your spouse. Thank God for him or her. Pray for one another, your kids, and any pressing needs. Close with each one of you saying The Marriage Prayer.

Make church a vital priority in your life. Many western Christians have gotten to the place where church is just one of many nice aspects of their lives. Some have no more allegiance to their church than their country club, alma mater, kid's school, or favorite vacation spot.

But God meant for the church to be so much more than that. The church should be a physical representation of the kingdom of God on Earth. It should be a dominant priority in our lives. Every Christian needs to have a significant place of involvement and service in their church. It's our chance to join God in bringing transformation to the lives of people in our community and the world.

I guess I can't do that by being a spectator for an hour a week.

You're right. Church is not a show to watch. The pastors and leaders are not there to make our lives pleasant and happy. We can't complain that they don't know our name, they didn't come see us when we were sick, or that they are going to let the youth group ruin the carpet. Church is not about who has the best singers or the most convenient parking.

A local church exists to see the gospel radically infect the lives of people who need Christ.

The church is the new temple and the place where God's presence and power touches earth. Paul clearly states that each of us is a vital part of the body of Christ through our church (1 Corinthians 12). We all have a part to play. A major reason we have so many anemic churches is that average members don't have a vision for how God can use them for His glory.

NBAS (No-Brainer Action Step)

If you are not strategically involved in your church, take a look this Sunday for a way to connect more deeply. Pray and ask God to guide you to your right next step. It can be a small step.

Spend time with God regularly and share what you are learning. Does the name Muhammad Saeed al-Sahhaf ring a bell? He was "Baghdad Bob," the Iraqi information minister during the U.S. invasion in 2003. Day after day he came on TV and made pronouncements about how well the war was going for the Iraqis. Finally, the day before Baghdad was under complete American control, he said this: "The Americans are not there. They're not in Baghdad. There are no troops there. Never. They're not at all." Unfortunately for him, news cameras around the corner from his press conference were filming the American convoy of tanks as they drove by a few hundred yards away.

The world is like "Baghdad Bob." It's bombarding us with "disinformation" all day long. It constantly lies to us about what will make us happy, where meaning comes from, and how we can have the kind of life we've always wanted. How do we counteract these lies?

Our minds must constantly be renewed by God's truth. "I wait for the Lord, my soul waits, and in his word I put my hope" (Psalm 130:5). God's truth in our only hope.

Some couples are at a stage of life where they are able to sit down together to read their Bibles and pray. Many others have schedules that make that difficult.

The important thing is that both of you are reading God's Word and talking together about what God is doing in your lives. We have never known anyone whose life has changed in any significant way apart from the regular study of God's Word. Read it in the morning or last thing before bed, get a devotional via e-mail, listen to it on CD or your iPod—just be sure that you are regularly ingesting the Word of God.

NBAS No-Brainer Action Step

Read the Bible today—choose a chapter in one of the Gospels if you don't know where to start. Sit down with your spouse and share one insight or reminder you saw in your reading.

A (Slightly Disguised) True Story about... Worship
John and Michelle (continued)

The lessons of their children's rebellion turned out to be preparation for what lay ahead. Due to deteriorating health, John was forced to take early retirement from his work. Now Michelle became not only wife, but also part-time care-giver.

The trust they had in God and each other allowed them to make these transitions. Because they knew that neither one would ever intentionally hurt the other, they could talk about anything.

As John's health continued to decline, they remained absolutely convinced of God's love for them as His children. They knew that God wouldn't give them more than they could handle.

True worship helped create a great marriage.

They always prayed that their marriage would be a light to others. Now that is happening in ways they could never have imagined. As people see their teamwork and faith, John and Michelle have the opportunity to share about what God has done for them. They often counsel other married couples and love to practice hospitality in their home. Even though they cannot go out to do ministry—God in His grace brings the ministry to them.

They continue to be amazed at God's faithfulness. After they were married a few years they got a chance to build a new home. They chose a plan with limited walls, large doorways, and no steps—not knowing that eventually John would require a home just like this. They may not have known, but God did, and He provided it just for them.

Worship as Renewal

Meet the Johnsons. They argued most of the way to church on Sunday morning. As soon as they got out of the car, the whole family put on their "Sunday Smiles." They sat in their standard pew. They breathed a sigh of relief, hoping to get filled up by God. The pastor preached, the congregation sang, they prayed, and by the time the worship service was over they felt renewed through worship. As they left the church, they had enough Jesus to at least begin the week.

But by the end of Monday, they were both down to three-quarters of a tank. By the time they make it through Tuesday's problems and Wednesday's challenges, they were less than half full. On Saturday morning, as they were carting the kids around, Mom and Dad were both running on empty. They moped around the rest of Saturday, then on Sunday loaded up the family and headed off to church. They were able to get within sight of the church building before they ran completely out of spiritual gas. They had enough momentum to coast into the parking lot where they parked, got out the car, trudged into church, plopped down, and said, "Okay, Pastor, fill us."

A lot of people go through this kind of weekly worship cycle. The problem is that weekly worship leads to weekly renewal. However frequently you choose to worship is how frequently you will be renewed. You get to decide the frequency of your worship, and you get to decide the frequency of your renewal.

Make worship a priority for your marriage. Don't allow the pace and distractions of modern life to define your existence. Break out of the mold to make sure you are regularly "putting on the glasses" of worship. Your life together should help clarify your spouse's view of God, so that both of you see Him for more of who He is. Cultivate together a lifestyle of acknowledging God in every aspect of your lives.

Then you'll see The Marriage Prayer become a reality—"Help me bring her into Your presence today."

CHAPTER REVIEW

This crossword puzzle contains many of the main concepts found in the chapter. Get with your spouse, find a watch or clock with a second hand, and see how long it takes to solve the entire puzzle. If you'd like, record your time here _____.

Are you reading the book with a group? See which couple had the fastest time the next time you are together. Reward that couple with a gift certificate, a pet lemur, or a collection of scented candles. (If you'd prefer to just see the answers, turn to the answer key on page 215.)

ACROSS

1   Acknowledging God
4   He said, "They aren't in the city."
8   Worship is like these for the soul.
9   It's raging for your heart.
10 Invest in it in a big way.
11 "righteous" "information," syn.

DOWN

2   _____ with your spouse
3   Power through His presence
5   "I can be good enough."
6   Weekly worship brings weekly _____.
7   This brother practiced the presence.

You Haven't Finished This Chapter Until. . .

Worship. Probably seemed like a weird chapter for a marriage book. Hopefully it doesn't seem so strange anymore. We hope it feels really important. So important that you'll take a few more minutes to allow God to cement these thoughts in your heart.

Please don't graduate to chapter 7 until . . .

☐ You've completed the exercises, including the Please Do Try This at Home (p. 111) and the No Brainer Action Steps (pp. 113, 114, 115 and 116).

☐ You are continuing the habit of saying The Marriage Prayer every day.

☐ You and your spouse have discussed the reflection questions below.

Questions for Reflection and Discussion

Use the questions to cement the ideas from this chapter into your marriage. Discuss them with your spouse and your small group of couples.

1. Before reading this chapter, would you have thought worship is a strange subject for a marriage book? Do you still feel that way? Why or why not?

2. What parts of the "True Story" could you most relate to? What aspects seem foreign? How could you apply some lesson to your marriage?

3. Read the big idea again. Does it seem like a big idea to you? Could it help your marriage? Why or why not?

4. Is there one step that you want to implement because of what you read and talked about in this chapter? If so, what is it and why do you want to do it?

A One-Hour Deposit for the Heart
Section 3: Purpose

Here's an exercise to help make your prayer—*Help me bring him (her) into Your presence today*—a reality. Take about ten minutes to think through the Psalm 19:7–14 and questions below. Then talk about your answers, knowing your discussion will bring your spouse closer to God. Close with a prayer asking God to continue to shape your hearts and minds to worship Him alone.

The law of the LORD is perfect,
   reviving the soul.
   The statutes of the LORD are trustworthy,
   making wise the simple.

The precepts of the LORD are right,
   giving joy to the heart.
   The commands of the LORD are radiant,
   giving light to the eyes.

What qualities are used to describe God's Word in these verses? Pick one to consider more deeply. How could you use more of that in your life?

The fear of the LORD is pure,
   enduring forever.
   The ordinances of the LORD are sure
   and altogether righteous.

They are more precious than gold,
   than much pure gold;
   they are sweeter than honey,
   than honey from the comb.

Looking back over the last few months, would you say you consider God's Word more precious than gold? Why or why not? What could that look like?

By them is your servant warned;
   in keeping them there is great reward.

Who can discern his errors?
   Forgive my hidden faults.

Keep your servant also from willful sins;
   may they not rule over me.
   Then will I be blameless,
   innocent of great transgression.

Two types of sins are described—those we are not aware of and those we knowingly commit. Which seems more difficult for you to deal with? Why?

May the words of my mouth and the
   meditation of my heart
   be pleasing in your sight,
   O LORD, my Rock and my Redeemer.

Conclude with a prayer together, letting this verse be an expression of the purpose God has for you.

Section 4: Unity

Ladies, let's keep praying the Marriage Prayer daily.

Father,

I said, "'Til death do us part"—I want to mean it.

Help me love You more than him,

and him more than anyone or anything else.

Help me bring him into Your presence today.

Make us one, like You are three in one.

Unity

I want to hear him, support him, and serve him—

so he would love You more and we can bring You glory.

Amen.

The next chapters are about UNITY. Most people today prize their independence. Our culture places a high value on being able to stand on your own two feet. We don't like the thought that we have to depend on anyone else.

Yet, in marriage, the Bible says that you are no longer your own. You have been united to your spouse. You belong to one another.

In the next two chapters, we'll examine two big ideas:

- ▶ **When God sees you and your spouse, He sees "one flesh."**
- ▶ **Physical intimacy is the by-product of many small sacrifices done with no ulterior motive.**

There are so many forces and distractions trying to pull you and your spouse apart. Use this next section of the book to reinforce your commitment to be "one flesh" before God. That only comes as God works in our hearts through faith.

That's why we pray in The Marriage Prayer, "Make us one, like you are three in one."

7: Oneness

Uniting Your Hearts

How well do you know your spouse? Let's find out by playing the following game. Grab two sheets of scrap paper—one for him and one for her. For each of the questions below, write down **how you think your spouse will answer**. Keep your answers hidden. Then ask your spouse the question to see if you were right. (If you're reading this with a group, give yourself 25 points for each correct answer, then compare your total score with the group. A perfect score would be 200 points. You may want to provide a free cruise or ski vacation to the winner.)

How will my spouse answer?

1. _____
2. _____
3. _____
4. _____

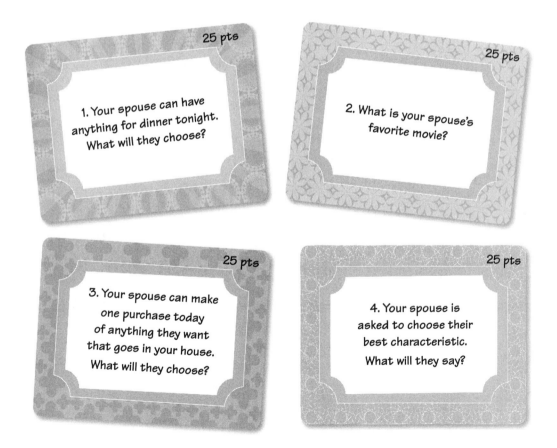

25 pts

1. Your spouse can have anything for dinner tonight. What will they choose?

25 pts

2. What is your spouse's favorite movie?

25 pts

3. Your spouse can make one purchase today of anything they want that goes in your house. What will they choose?

25 pts

4. Your spouse is asked to choose their best characteristic. What will they say?

RULES OF ENGAGEMENT

Discuss your answers for a few minutes. Which answer was the biggest surprise? Why?

◆

A (Slightly Disguised) True Story about…Oneness
Jeremy and Amanda

At 2 o'clock in the morning, with suitcases spread all over the bedroom floor, Jeremy turned to Amanda. "There is no way we're going on this trip like this. Let's just cancel the tickets and stay home."

Amanda was stunned. She looked up from the suitcase she was working on, hand still on the zipper. "What do you mean, 'Cancel the tickets'? It's our spring break."

Jeremy sat down on the edge of the bed. "It doesn't matter—we've been fighting all week, and now we've been fighting all night, and I'm not going away for a week with the kids and then fight all the time."

Amanda and Jeremy have been married for fifteen years. They'd planned a special trip for their family and Amanda's parents. Jeremy travels regularly for business, so they'd used their frequent flyer points to schedule a fun and educational trip to New England. Their kids were really excited about the trip, but the way their last week had gone, neither of them felt very much like spending a week together.

To be continued…

If you've ever seen the movie *The Princess Bride*, you probably remember the scene where the highly dignified and ornately dressed clergyman clears his throat and says, "Mawage, that bwessed awangment, that dweam wifin a dweam..." We all know marriage doesn't always feel like a blessed arrangement or a dream within a dream. We are fallen, imperfect people—with all our warts and failings—living together under one roof. We get on each other's nerves. We have to deal with different opinions and perspectives. Our best actions often end up falling short of our spouse's, or our own, lofty expectations.

But all this just makes what God does in marriage even more amazing—even miraculous. And when we pray, "Make us one, like You are three in one," we are getting to the very core of this miracle: in marriage, **God takes two separate people and makes them one.**

Pat Morley's mom and dad had been married fifty-four years when it became obvious that Pat's mother was fading fast. A few weeks before she died, Pat talked to her and his father about the future. They had a discussion about where his father would live. Pat and his mother wanted to keep his dad in their home but were afraid that due to his infirmity he couldn't manage the household. They asked him, "Dad, where do you want to live?"

Typical of his stoicism and unselfishness, he said, "I don't really care." They kept pressing, and after a few repetitions of the same answer, he looked at Pat's mom and said, "I don't care. I just want to be with you." In marriage, through selfless love, God makes us one.

Nothing else on earth is quite like it.

What This Oneness Is All About

The miracle of marriage is grounded in the nature of God Himself. He is three persons—Father, Son, and Holy Spirit—in one essence. There's an eternal relationship of love, communication, purpose, and intimacy between the persons of the God-head. God has never known a single moment when He was alone without this tri-unity.

But when He created man, He made a single person. So man cannot fully express the image of God in isolation. This is why God said, "It is not good for man to be alone." We need to be in relationship with others.

When you connect with a friend to deal with significant issues, or to laugh, or to pray, or to cry—you know that something deep and real is happening there.

You're right. It's not like watching a sitcom on TV, buying a new sofa, or playing a round of golf.

And it's not even just a quantitative difference; it's a qualitative difference. It's a totally different thing. Why? Because it resonates with the part of us made in the image of God. The bonding that occurs when we connect with the soul of another person reflects the experience that God Himself has among Father, Son, and the Holy Spirit.

Why Marriage Is So Special

This is why marriage is so special and sacred. As the most intimate human relationship, marriage is a laboratory for us to express this relational character of God.

And from a practical perspective, your destiny has been intertwined with that of your spouse. You've become one flesh. If something happens to one of you, it happens to both of you. The famous T-shirt is correct, "If Mama ain't happy, ain't nobody happy." You've been melded together by the power of God.

If marriage was simply two people living together, divorce would not have many consequences. You probably had roommates in college or when you were younger, and you eventually went your separate ways. It may have been sad, but it wasn't that big a deal. If marriage is nothing but convenience, physical pleasure, not being alone, or having somebody help take care of you, why is divorce so devastating?

For those of you reading this book who've been through divorce, you know the pain, the heartache, and how deep that division feels in your soul. It feels like you have had a part of yourself ripped away—because you have.

In marriage, God intertwines you and your spouse together so that your destinies cannot be separated.

How Is This Oneness Accomplished?

How does God make two people one? Paul links oneness in marriage to the biblical idea of "headship" or "representation." This may sound like a foreign concept, but you already know more about this than you think.

Is the United States technically a democracy? No, we have a representative form of government. Every individual doesn't vote on every issue. We elect people to represent us, then those people vote, and their vote counts as our vote. That's political representation. Where did our founding fathers get that idea?

House of Representatives

It came from the Bible. The Bible talks about two representatives of the human race (Romans 5).

The First Representative: Adam	**The Second Representative: Jesus**
Every person is born "in Adam." Because Adam is our representative, when he sinned, we sinned. When Adam fell, we all fell, and we suffer the consequences of his sin.	There is a "second Adam" ordained by God—Jesus Christ. All those who put their faith and trust in Him are represented by Him. He suffered the wrath of God for us.

If you've never come to Jesus Christ by faith, you are still united with Adam and living under the curse of sin. But, if you believe in Jesus Christ, you now have a new representative, a new head. And you are united with Him. His actions are attributed to us. So we get the benefit of His death on our behalf, but we also benefit from His righteous, perfect life. His obedience brings life to us (Romans 5:19).

By his power God raised the Lord from the dead, and he will raise us also. Do you not know that your bodies are members of Christ himself? Shall I then take the members of Christ and unite them with a prostitute? Never! Do you not know that he who unites himself with a prostitute is one with her in body?

A physical union with Christ

A spiritual union with Christ

For it is said, "The two will become one flesh." But he who unites himself with the Lord is one with him in spirit. (1 Corinthians 6:14–17)

The apostle Paul says we are both physically and spiritually united with Christ. If we are in Christ, both our spirits and our bodies are one day going to be restored (1 Corinthians 15). They're going to be remade and renewed.

How can you tell your body was united to Adam and was involved in his sin? Have you looked in the mirror lately? Imagine some pictures of you from five or ten years ago. Illness, disease, deformities, aging, death—our bodies wear out because our bodies are affected by Adam's sin. It's not just a spiritual union with Adam or with Christ. We are a united being, spirit and body.

Why is that important? The great marriage story of all history has Christ as the bride-groom and us as His bride in the church. Marriage was designed by God to be a picture of Christ's love for the church. It represents what Christ has done for His people.

So God unites a man and a woman bodily and spiritually in the same way that He has united Christ and the church. When we experience the unity of marriage on earth, it reflects the unity of our relationship with God through Jesus Christ. And it represents the eternal unity of the Trinity. What a high calling God gives us in marriage! That's why we pray, "Make us one, like You are three in one."

The **Big** Idea

When God sees you and your spouse, He sees "one flesh."

A (Slightly Disguised) True Story about…Oneness
Jeremy and Amanda (continued)

A few weeks earlier Jeremy had returned from a week-long business trip. It had been a stressful time for Amanda and the kids while he was gone. As Jeremy was settling in his first night back at home, Amanda confided in him, "I'm emotionally empty, and I've felt like this for six months."

Jeremy was bewildered. He hadn't known anything was going on, and he sure didn't know what Amanda expected him to do about it. As they talked about her feelings, she indicated she wanted Jeremy to "pursue her again." She had a hard time explaining to Jeremy what that looked like. The more she said it, the more frustrated and angry he became. She finally mentioned things like sitting close to her on the couch, holding her hand, and rolling over to talk to her before they went to sleep.

Over the next week—the week before their spring break trip—Jeremy tried to consciously show his love for Amanda. He was intentional about "working her list" and doing the things she had asked of him. But as they talked while packing for their trip, she told him that it felt like he was just doing these things out of duty and obligation. She didn't want him to do these things because he had to, but because he wanted to.

Jeremy just sat down on the edge of the bed and stared.

To be continued…

Has this ever happened to you?

Barriers to Oneness

Our fallen world makes experiencing oneness difficult. So many things are stacked against us. The pace of life, our selfish desires, temptations, preconceptions, and worldly values—all these things can destroy unity in our marriage. As a rule, barriers to oneness occur when we react to situations by choosing to **pull apart** rather than **draw together**.

Every interaction a couple has will either draw them closer together or push them apart. Each individual interaction may not have much impact, but multiplied by hundreds of interactions each month and thousands of interactions each year, it begins to add up.

Each time you pull away from your spouse you are adding to a downward spiral. Each time you choose to connect and engage, you are reversing that trend and growing the oneness in your marriage.

Here's a great example. Many women have a core desire to be pursued and cherished. At the same time, many men try to avoid conflict. In a lot of marriages, these two values collide.

So when a woman is feeling down or dealing with an emotionally difficult situation, she wants a man to be proactive in demonstrating his love for her. At the same time, most men shrink away from unknown situations where they aren't sure what to do or how things will turn out. And for many men, willingly walking into an emotionally-charged situation with their wife definitely qualifies as an unknown outcome. ☺

What does this look like in real life? See if this sounds familiar.

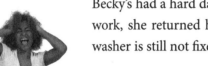

Becky's had a hard day. The kids have been crazy, the garage door wouldn't work, she returned home from soccer practice in the rain, and the dishwasher is still not fixed from when it stopped working last week.

Jim comes home from work and they have a quiet dinner with the kids. After dinner, their son Tommy ignores his mom's request to get in the shower and Becky erupts. "I AM SO TIRED OF BEING IGNORED AROUND HERE. WHEN I TELL YOU TO GET IN THE SHOWER I MEAN NOW!" Jim gets up and ushers Tommy to the shower, knowing that something's not right.

When Jim asks Becky what's wrong, she forcefully replies: "What's wrong? What do you mean, what's wrong? You can't see WHAT'S WRONG?!!" Jim loves his wife. He hates to see her hurting. And he also wants the conflict and anger to end.

So Jim and Becky have a choice:

▌ Becky can sharpen her quills like an angry porcupine, but then she'll be wondering why Jim won't pursue her.

▌ Jim can try to avoid conflict at all costs, wait it out and hope it blows over, but then he'll wonder why Becky grows cold and distant.

Both of these approaches are barriers to oneness.

A woman has to allow a man to be close to her when she is angry and frustrated. A man has to fight through his desire to avoid conflict, to always be right, or to find a quick fix, and instead be there for his wife.

We understand that in many marriages, these roles are reversed some or all of the time. But in any case, both parties have to make the commitment to fight for one another's hearts no matter the circumstances.

Okay, it's time to get specific, real, and practical about your circumstances.

PLEASE DO TRY THIS AT HOME

Has there been a time when you were tempted to pull away from your spouse? What is a situation that made you draw together? Share your insights with one another.

Becoming One Means Being Other-Centered

While we will never experience perfect oneness on earth, marriage is an opportunity to give ourselves away fully to another person. The primary way to overcome barriers to oneness in your marriage is to be other-centered. Christ's love for the church is sacrificial. Paul essentially said to husbands, "Love your wife in the same way that Christ loves the church. You should be willing to give yourself up for her." (Eph. 5:25)

Most of us won't have to step in front of a bullet for our spouses, but we might very well have to take a paintball now and then. When our desire is to lash out, punish, or ignore—we need to remember the prayer, "Make us one, like You are three in one." Instead of pushing away and perpetuating a downward spiral, we need to extend grace and take small positive steps.

We all do. The truth is this: We will draw together rather than pull apart when we really believe that **loving our spouse is loving ourself**.

Why does the Bible say we should lay aside our own agendas and deny ourselves? For the same reason that Christ loved the church. Christ loved the church sacrificially to present her as a beautiful bride to God. In the same way, God has given us a unique opportunity to help our spouses become everything God wants them to be. In an environment where we lay our lives down for them, they are nourished and they can flourish.

Paul reveals the logic of this when he says, "He who loves his wife loves himself" (Ephesians 5:28).

It's tempting to read this as, "A man should love his wife like he's loving himself."

But Paul goes farther than that. He basically said, "He who loves his wife **is loving himself**." When we love our spouses, we are loving ourselves. Our union is so powerful and so real that when we sacrificially love our spouses, we really are loving ourselves. That's what we were made for. That's the way we find the greatest joy and satisfaction. We were wired to create oneness by giving ourselves away for our spouses.

Becoming One by Investing Time

Unfortunately, couples are often trying to work out all the kinks in the marriage knot at the same time they are also establishing careers, a home, and a family. That makes developing oneness even harder.

Let's do a little analysis. If you sleep for eight hours each night, you will have 960 waking minutes each day.

By the time you are finished with getting ready, work, chores, children, exercise, eating, your commute and a few minutes of downtime—there's not much left for you and your spouse.

Here's the question: Would you be willing to give your spouse 2 percent of your waking hours each day? What would that look like? About twenty minutes.

Find a way to invest twenty minutes each day into the emotional and spiritual health of your spouse. Set aside twenty minutes in the morning for coffee. Or, twenty minutes in the morning to discuss the day ahead, then pray together. Or, after dinner, stick around the table for about twenty minutes and just be with one another. There is no way to experience oneness without investing in one another.

At the thirteen-year-mark in his marriage, Pat calculated that eleven of their couple friends were either separated or getting divorced. As he pondered this staggering revelation, he realized that Patsy was not his top priority after God. He viewed her basically as someone to help him achieve his dreams. He'd not considered that she might have a dream of her own. And then it hit him: he was using her. He felt dirty and ashamed, which led to genuine repentance. But he didn't know what to do—practically speaking.

Pat asked God to show him what to do. A plan began to take shape to make Patsy his best friend. After dinner, Pat started to linger at the dinner table. No agenda. Just to be with Patsy. For about twenty minutes each day, he would ask about her day, her dreams, her fears, her hopes, her concerns. He'd ask how the children were doing from her perspective.

One day a few weeks later, Pat came home from work and there was a plaque on the counter next to the bathroom sink. It says, "Happiness is being married to your best friend."

That was over twenty years ago, but he still proudly displays the "Happiness" plaque in his office. It reminds him of God's love, mercy, and grace.

NBAS (No-Brainer Action Step)

What is something you could do together with your twenty minutes? Decide now to try it tomorrow.

Love and Oneness

In his book *The Four Loves*, C.S. Lewis describes four different varieties of love—*affection*, *friendship*, *eros*, and *charity*. First, affection is the kind of love that simply enjoys the company of our mate. Second, friendship is what happens when you and your spouse connect because of a common interest. Third, eros is the kind of love we are talking about when we say we are "in love." Fourth, charity is selfless love that mimics the love of God.

Lewis makes two very interesting points about eros and charity. For eros, Lewis says that it is about more than sex. Sexual desire, without true eros, just wants sex. In contrast, Eros wants the beloved. "Now Eros makes a man want, not just a woman, but one particular woman. In some mysterious but quite indisputable fashion, the lover desires the beloved herself, not the pleasure she can give."[1] In other words, "It's not sex that I want, I want you. I want to experience true oneness with another human being. I want to know you and be known by you." That's what eros is all about.

---

1. C. S. Lewis, *The Four Loves* (New York: Harcourt, 1991), 135.

Lewis describes charity as "Gift-love" that reflects the divine love God has for us. Gift-love is love that provides solely for the benefit of others and does not seek anything for itself. Through Christ, God gives us the ability to express this selfless love to others. And in the mystery of marriage, we both **need** to be loved with charity by our spouse, and we have the ability to **give** charity to our spouse. We experience a profound oneness through selfless love.

Tom and Susan are both in their mideighties and are now reaping the benefits of a lifetime of charity toward each another. They can't get out much anymore, so their world has shrunk. Most of their time is spent at home with each another.

When you are with them the atmosphere of love and oneness is palpable. They care for each other tenderly. Tom makes sure Susan has taken her medicine. Susan helps Tom with his oxygen after he has been up and around for too long. They pray together regularly and still talk about what God is teaching them through His Word.

They are enjoying the precious reward of what we pray when we say, "Make us one, like You are three in one."

A (Slightly Disguised) True Story about…Oneness
Jeremy and Amanda (continued)

That night, sitting on the edge of the bed, Jeremy felt completely trapped. If he didn't do anything, Amanda said she felt empty. If he did the things she asked him to do, that didn't count either. He never did really understand what she meant by "pursuing her," and so far their heated discussions weren't helping. No matter what he did he felt like he couldn't "win" at this game.

Amanda wanted to feel connected to Jeremy again. She couldn't explain all the reasons why she didn't feel connected right now, but

Can you relate to what they are feeling?

she just didn't. She needed him to listen to her, empathize with her frustrations, and demonstrate his love for her. The fact that he didn't recognize and understand her needs infuriated her. That short night was one of the longest in their marriage.

No, they didn't cancel the trip. But it wasn't easy either. A cloud of tension surrounded them for several days. Even after they came home they struggled with how to understand their feelings and truly serve one another.

These unresolved issues continue to be a frontline battlefield in their relationship; they haven't found any quick answers. But one issue that is resolved—their absolute commitment to love one other and make their marriage work.

G. K. Chesterson wrote about the mystery of oneness in his book *Orthodoxy,* one of the most important books of the twentieth century. In the early 1900s in England, many young men revolted against the idea of monogamy. Chesterton made the point that he was willing to obey any rule when the mystery of what he gained was so much greater than the mystery of the rule. He said this, "Keeping to one woman is a small price for so much as seeing one woman."[2]

He goes on to say, "To complain that I could only be married once is like complaining that I'd only been born once." A woman is a glorious thing. (And the same could be said for a man.) It's an inestimable privilege to be one with your spouse in marriage.

What an incredible gift God has given you in your mate. Seek oneness with your spouse this week. Draw together, don't pull apart. Don't leave this chapter until you've taken some steps to bring the prayer into reality: "Make us one, like You are three in one."

---

2. *The Collected Works of G. K. Chesterton,* (San Francisco, CA, Ignatius Press, 1986). p. 261.

CHAPTER REVIEW

Unscramble the following words and phrases to find the letters that form the big idea from Chapter 7. Use the numbers to match the letters.

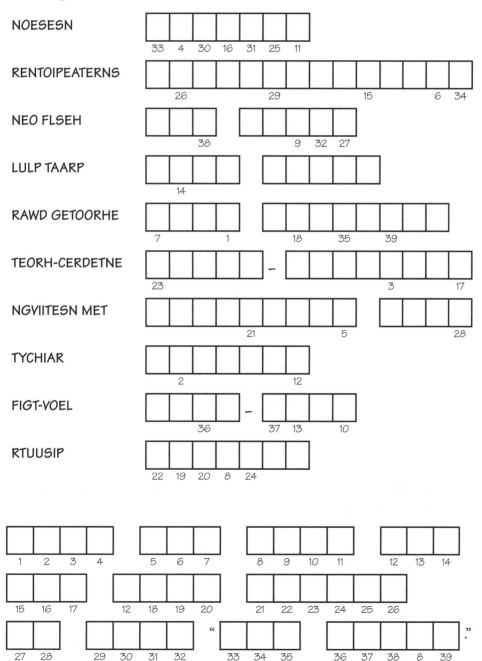

NOESESN

33 4 30 16 31 25 11

RENTOIPEATERNS

26 29 15 6 34

NEO FLSEH

38 9 32 27

LULP TAARP

14

RAWD GETOORHE

7 1 18 35 39

TEORH-CERDETNE

23 3 17

NGVIITESN MET

21 5 28

TYCHIAR

2 12

FIGT-VOEL

36 37 13 10

RTUUSIP

22 19 20 8 24

1 2 3 4   5 6 7   8 9 10 11   12 13 14

15 16 17   12 18 19 20   21 22 23 24 25 26

27 28   29 30 31 32   " 33 34 35   36 37 38 8 39 "

You Haven't Finished This Chapter Until...

Oneness is complicated in theory and complicated in practice. Let God do whatever He wants to do in your heart and life. Your marriage is worth it, and so is His glory.

So, make sure that...

❏ You've completed the exercises, including the Please Do Try This at Home (p. 133) and the No-Brainer Action Step (p. 136)

❏ You've memorized The Marriage Prayer or posted it somewhere so that you are saying it every day.

❏ You've discussed the reflection questions with your spouse.

Questions for Reflection and Discussion

1. Before reading this chapter, had you spent much time thinking about oneness in marriage? What was your view? Has it changed as a result of reading the chapter?

2. Which aspects of the "True Story" rang true for you? What lesson from the story could you apply to your marriage?

3. Consider the big idea from this chapter. How should we be influenced by how God thinks of us? What difference does that make?

4. What practical step are you taking away from this chapter? How will you go about making it a reality?

8: Sex

Becoming One Flesh

Here's a quick question to keep things moving. Which words below reflect some aspect of your sexual relationship?

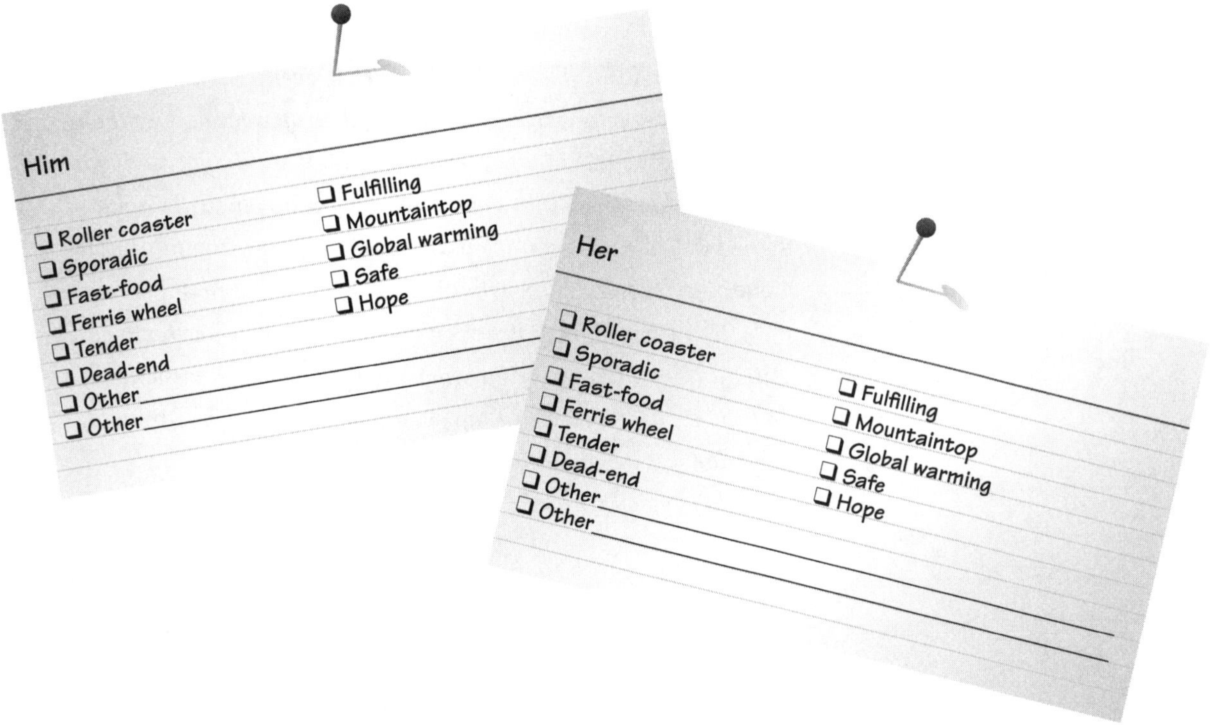

Him

- ❏ Roller coaster
- ❏ Sporadic
- ❏ Fast-food
- ❏ Ferris wheel
- ❏ Tender
- ❏ Dead-end
- ❏ Other_____
- ❏ Other_____

- ❏ Fulfilling
- ❏ Mountaintop
- ❏ Global warming
- ❏ Safe
- ❏ Hope

Her

- ❏ Roller coaster
- ❏ Sporadic
- ❏ Fast-food
- ❏ Ferris wheel
- ❏ Tender
- ❏ Dead-end
- ❏ Other_____
- ❏ Other_____

- ❏ Fulfilling
- ❏ Mountaintop
- ❏ Global warming
- ❏ Safe
- ❏ Hope

RULES OF ENGAGEMENT

Talk with your spouse about the words you checked. Were there any surprises?

◆

A (Slightly Disguised) True Story about…Sex
Brandon and Lauren

Brandon gazed through the dim light of the bedroom at his wife's profile. Beside him in the bed, Lauren lay weeping, quietly facing the wall. Only having been married three months, Brandon had no idea what to do.

It had started out well. They'd spent the evening with some friends having dinner and watching a movie. After they got back to their apartment, they spent a few minutes talking as they got ready for bed. Brandon hoped that tonight would lead to physical intimacy, so he made a casual comment as they were getting in to bed. "Hey honey—are you thinking what I'm thinking?" Lauren didn't respond.

After they lay down, Brandon rolled over to give Lauren a kiss. After a brief moment, he attempted to kiss her more passionately, but she broke it off, turned her head, and rolled away. Confused, Brandon put his hands behind his head and waited.

That's when he heard Lauren begin to quietly sob.

To be continued…

Have you ever experienced something like this?

There are few things in marriage that have the potential to bring as much joy as sex. Let's face it, if sex wasn't a lot of fun, it wouldn't be such a big deal.

There are also few things in marriage that have such potential to bring as much pain and devastation as sex. You know people who, for a few moments of pleasure, have devastated their lives. What they worked for—a marriage and family they cherished for five, ten, fifteen, or twenty years—they threw it all away for a few moments of pleasure. That's how powerful sex is.

Why is sex such an area of struggle for so many couples? You don't need this book to tell you that we live in a sex-saturated culture. It's everywhere—on televisions, computer screens, billboards, magazines, even in mall advertisements. It's a major driving force in our economy. Sex sells.

We see two different erroneous responses in our culture today.

1 Some religious people are afraid of sex. They treat it as taboo, evil, dirty, and bad. They believe sex shouldn't be discussed. It's something you just have to hide, tolerate, or endure.

2 The more prevalent tendency today sees sex as just like any other activity. It's for pleasure. You do it as much as you can. This flows from a belief in evolution and humanism. We're just animals with animal instincts, and it's survival of the fittest, so just go and have as much fun as possible.

PLEASE DO TRY THIS AT HOME

Answer this question with your spouse. How did you learn about the birds and the bees? What were you taught?

I know what our culture says. But what is sex really?

We actually have to get theological to answer your question. That may surprise you, but you can't understand sex if you don't understand theology. This probably isn't part of the Sex Ed 101 that they are teaching in middle school. But it's true.

Why? In the deepest sense theology is life. We can't understand the world unless we understand the God who made it. We can't cut ourselves off from our source and expect to make sense of reality. The devastation we see today in the area of sexuality is a direct result of people divorcing themselves from the truth of God.

So what is sex? Building on what we wrote in the last chapter, the Bible says sex represents something incredibly important to who we are as people made in the image of God (1 Corinthians 6:13–18).

God made us for relationships. Once we are a Christian, we are "in Christ" and united to Him in a deep relationship. In terms of human relationships, the closest we can possibly have is the union we experience as husband and wife.

> The Lord God made a woman from the rib he had taken out of the man and he brought her to the man.
>
> The man said, "This is now bone of my bones, flesh of my flesh; she shall be called 'woman,' for she was taken out of man." For this reason a man will leave his father and mother and be united to his wife, and they will become one flesh.
>
> The man and his wife were both naked, and they felt no shame. (Genesis 2:22–25)

When Jesus quoted this passage He added to it, "What God has joined together, let not man separate" (Matthew 19:6). So He affirms this profound unity.

This union is a spiritual oneness. But it's also a physical union, because in the garden they became one flesh, and in their nakedness there was no shame. There was a physical intimacy without any barriers whatsoever. Of course, now we live after the fall, and there are lots of barriers and impediments to physical intimacy.

We saw in the last chapter that marriage is a laboratory for us to express the relational character of the Trinity. God is three in one—through sex He allows us to experience a taste of what it is like to be physically two in one. He awakens things in us through sex that we don't experience any other way. This is why we say in The Marriage Prayer, "Make us one, like You are three in one."

Sex is so wonderful because it is a physical fulfillment of that prayer to "make us one."

That's right, sex is not just an ordinary activity.

Why do people who treat sex as something casual and fun outside of marriage wake up in the morning and say, "What in the world have I done?" Evolution has no explanation for those feelings. The Scriptures do. Not only have we violated our marriage relationship, we've violated our union with Christ, and we've also violated something special about the image of God in us. So sex can be incredibly wonderful, but it can also be incredibly dangerous.

How to Keep Sex in Its Place—ACT

Before we talk about how to have great sex, we want to help you avoid pitfalls. Here are three simple ideas (which form the acrostic ACT) to help keep sex where it belongs in your marriage.

A **Avoid temptation.** "Flee the evil desires of youth, and pursue righteousness" (2 Timothy 2:22). "Do not think about how to gratify the desires of the sinful nature" (Romans 13:14). **Make a plan and take practical steps to avoid temptation.** Many men reading this book are struggling with pornography. Your spouse may not even know. Some of you travel. You know what it's like to turn on the TV in a lonely hotel room late at night. Make decisions now that will help you stay pure later.

You may be working closely with someone whom you're attracted to. She jokes with you. He seems to really care. Take steps now to put some distance between you. Make these decisions quickly, before the thrill and excitement kick in. It's much easier to do it now than later.

Accountability is another key to resisting temptation. Isolation leaves us vulnerable. Take the area of pornography. Wife, you know that your husband is aroused by what he sees. It shouldn't be a shock to you that it excites him to see a naked or almost naked woman. That's not a huge revelation. But he may feel like he can't share his struggles with you. (He's probably afraid you'll think he's comparing you to them or that he values you less. For most men, it's not this at all—they are tempted by the momentary thrill and their fleshly desires.)

He's also hesitant to share his struggle with other men—even though they won't be surprised. So with his isolation comes the risk of falling. As men, we think that nobody knows. (Of course, God does, but we forget that.) All of us need to find someone to keep us accountable, a person we allow to ask us tough questions. And we need to give our spouse permission as well. As a husband and wife, you'll have a lot more joy if you realize that you are in this together.

Another principle for avoiding temptation: Don't go any farther than you've already gone. In every area of our lives it's always easier to go right up against the line of where you've been before. Keep those boundaries in place, whatever it takes. If you've never looked at an Internet site, avoid it at all costs. If you've never been alone in the office of that man or woman who seems so nice, keep it as a rule you just won't violate.

Todd was attracted to Julie at work. One day he was alone in a car with her after a business lunch. They ended up sharing a kiss. A few weeks later they consummated their relationship in a motel room, devastating their families and ruining their careers.

Stay as far away from crossing the line as you can. Every time you take another step, it's just that much easier to keep going.

C **Consider the consequences.** Satan loves to show you the bait and hide the hook. Perhaps you've experienced this, or you've seen it with others. With sex, people make a stupid, impulsive choice—they take the bait—and then the dominoes start falling with their families, their work, and with their church. They've been caught by the hook. And most often the damaging consequences go on for years.

Frankly, from the outside it's easy to think, *How could anybody have been so stupid? Didn't they think about what this would mean?* No, they thought, *I'll never get caught* or *It's just this one time.* That's the whole point. We get caught up in the rush, the thrill—when the hormones, the adrenaline take over and we don't consider the consequences of our sins. That's what Satan wants us to do. He wants us to focus on short-term pleasure and forget about the long-term pain.

Most of us won't fall into some kind of devastating sexual sin in an instant. It's just not that easy to have an affair—it takes a lot of deception and planning. If it happens, it will spring from a long series of small decisions like water dripping on a rock. Each of those decisions involves taking the bait and ignoring the hook.

Every summer David's family goes crabbing at the beach. They take twine and a chicken neck and throw it out into the surf. A crab finds the chicken, latches on, and starts chewing. The person with the twine slowly begins winding it back in toward shore. The crab doesn't think anything of this, because it's accustomed to the waves and tide pushing it back and forth. Slowly, but surely, they wind it in, until finally they dip the net and pull up the crab.

We are like that crab. We find something we want, something that gives us a little thrill, something that feels good, something we "deserve" because of how things are at home, something that starts our engine running, and then we latch on to it.

It seems like just a little thing. It's just a funny conversation with this nice person at work. Maybe it's just lingering over a magazine ad. A little channel surfing around the cable. Maybe it's just sharing a few emotional moments with a stranger on the Internet. A few drinks after work with the guys. It's just a little thing. Right? But we latch on, and Satan starts walking us in, one small step at a time.

We don't really notice any big changes. There's no one moment where we say, "This is finally the time that I'm going to do it." But ultimately we end up sitting there captured in Satan's net, and we wonder, "How in the world did I get here?"

James writes, "Each one is tempted when, by his own evil desire, he is dragged away and enticed. Then, after desire has conceived, it gives birth to sin, and sin, when it is full-grown, gives birth to death" (James 1:14–15).

A few years ago, Alex came to Pat and told him that he had been flirting with a woman on the Internet, and now she wanted to come see him in Orlando. He asked Pat, "What do I do?" Pat told him that God was giving him a chance to save his marriage and to tell her absolutely not. Fortunately, he dropped the bait before Satan could snare him.

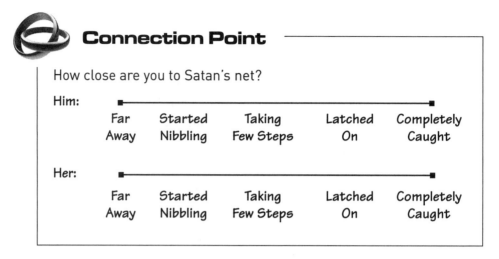

Connection Point

How close are you to Satan's net?

Him:

Far Away	Started Nibbling	Taking Few Steps	Latched On	Completely Caught

Her:

Far Away	Started Nibbling	Taking Few Steps	Latched On	Completely Caught

We really need to consider the consequences of any sexual immorality. Ask this question before God—"If this went on for six months, or a year, or five years, where would I naturally end up? Where is this thing headed?" Pray for the strength to walk away from the temptation. Consider the consequences of your sin.

Turn to Christ. When it comes to temptation, ask yourself, "Why am I more drawn to this sin than I am to Christ? What do I think that this sin will do for me that Jesus Christ can't do?" This is how we get to the root of our sin. We can avoid video stores, cut off the cable, get an Internet filter, move to a new neighborhood, even change jobs, but if we don't get to the root of it, sin will still fester in our heart.

A few years ago, David owned an eight-year-old van that ran pretty well. But it had a lot of small spots where the paint was chipped and rust had started to form. What would have happened if David just painted over those spots? That rust would continue to eat away until eventually it reappeared.

That's often what we try to do about our sin. We say, "I can stop this bad behavior. I'm going to get some accountability. I'm getting an Internet filter. I'm hiding the remote in the hotel room. I'm not going to walk by his office anymore."

None of these is a bad idea, but if that's all we do then we are painting over the surface and not dealing with the real issue. If we don't deal with the root issue of what's going on in our hearts, then ultimately it will show itself somewhere else. It's just like the rust on David's van. You have to dig down, treat it, grind it all out, and then you can restore the vehicle to its original condition.

So when dealing with sin, go ahead and put all those practical steps in place, but only as part of a process for dealing with the root issues in your heart. We need to go on the offensive, not just the defensive.

Our sinful actions flow from desires that we are not satisfying in Christ. That's why the Bible calls sin deceitful; because it lies to us. The world says "This pleasure is going to be so great. It's going to make you so happy." Or, "You deserve this, you're under so much stress." Or, "Your husband doesn't deserve sex—he hasn't been kind and considerate enough." These are all lies. The only way to really believe the truth is if we daily turn to Christ and see Him for who He is. "Satisfy us in the morning with your steadfast love that we may rejoice and be glad all our days" (Psalm 90:14 ESV).

WHY IS THIS SO IMPORTANT?

Both of these phenomena work on the exact same physical principle.

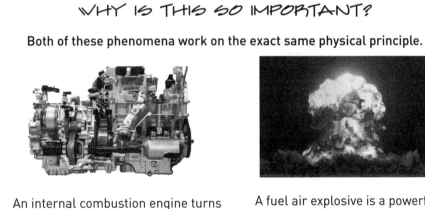

An internal combustion engine turns gasoline into a vapor which then explodes, forcing a piston to move thousands of times a minute.

A fuel air explosive is a powerful bomb that detonates a charge inside a vapor cloud of fuel.

An explosion of fuel is a wonderful thing in the right environment, under control, and at the proper time. But when it occurs outside of the boundaries of an engine, it causes devastation.

Sex is exactly the same way. When sex escapes the boundaries God made, it becomes a raging inferno that will destroy us.

◆

A (Slightly Disguised) True Story about…Sex
Brandon and Lauren (continued)

Like most men, Brandon went into marriage with high expectations for their sex life. He pictured nights of steamy romance and exhausted fulfillment.

Lauren, on the other hand, didn't know what to think. As a pre-teen she'd been abused by an older boy. Then she'd been involved with a series of guys in high school who used her and treated her like dirt. She brought a lot of baggage into her marriage.

Brandon knew about the abuse and the boyfriends before they got married. But he had no idea how hard it would be.

Not only did Lauren have a lot of emotional hurdles to overcome, she also experienced physical pain and discomfort during inter-course. Even when they were intimate, Brandon often felt like it was "pity sex"—that Lauren was enduring it to accommodate him. Too many times he let his frustration show as he pressured Lauren to do and feel things she wasn't ready for.

Lauren felt like a failure for not enjoying sex. Brandon felt like a failure because he had a wife who didn't like having sex with him. They couldn't talk about it—there was so much pain and frustration they didn't even know where to start.

To be continued…

> What aspect of your sexual relationship has brought the greatest frustration?

How to Have Great Sex

How can you and your spouse experience what God designed for you in the area of sexuality? Building on what we saw in the last chapter about "gift-love," consider the words of Jesus: "Then Jesus said to his disciples, 'If anyone would come after me, he must deny himself and take up his cross and follow me. For whoever wants to save his life will lose it, but whoever loses his life for me will find it'" (Matthew 16: 24–25).

That's a great verse. But, um, exactly what does it have to do with sex?

We're glad you asked.

In this saying, Jesus sums up the paradox of the gospel. Jesus is trying to show us that the values of the world are upside down in so many ways.

As we noted in chapter 1, if we believe we are on our own we think we have to take care of ourselves. So our natural focus is on providing for ourselves, trying to do those things that make us happy, that make us secure, and that make us comfortable. This is the natural inclination of a person's heart who doesn't have a relationship with God.

Jesus couldn't be any more radical than He is in this passage. He might as well have said that up is down and down is up. **Jesus says that trying to please yourself is actually the absolute wrong step you can take.** If you focus on yourself, in the end you're going to lose your life. Ironically, if we give ourselves away for the sake of Jesus, He says that in the end we find more life than we could have ever dreamed.

You've probably already verified this experientially. At some point in your life you served or sacrificed for someone else, and you got back in return the satisfaction, the joy, the reality that this was something good and real and right.

Jesus is actually just restating His greatest principle—"Love the Lord your God with all your heart, soul, mind and strength and love your neighbor as yourself." The gospel shows us that our new heart lives out of an "other" focus—God first, then others.

Of course the message of our culture is that "it's all about me." It's all about my being happy, about having the things I want, about my providing for myself. Especially in the area of sexuality, our culture constantly sells fantasies about how to find sexual fulfillment and how to use sex to get our way.

But that's not what Jesus says. He says built into the very fabric of what it means to be truly human and in the image of God is that you should be "others" focused, that you should love God with your whole heart and love others as yourself.

These weren't just pretty words for Jesus. He lived them out as a sacrifice for His people. He died a brutal death, suffering the wrath of God the Father against sin.

But why did Jesus do this? "Let us fix our eyes on Jesus, the author and perfecter of our faith, who *for the joy set before him* endured the cross, scorning its shame, and sat down at the right hand of the throne of God" (Hebrews 12:2, emphasis ours).

Why did Jesus endure the shame and die on the cross? "For the joy set before him." There's the paradox of the gospel. When you lose your life, you find it again.

What does all this have to do with having great sex? Your sex life will only be truly great when you understand how this paradox applies to marriage.

It's just an item on the list. (A very important item, but an item nonetheless. ☺)

There are lots of differences between men and women in the area of sex. For men, sex is often seen as a task or an activity, like something on a checklist.

But for women, it's not that way. For women, sexuality is a process. It's a long series of words and activities and interactions that culminate in sex. Sometimes it's hard to understand our spouse's perspective.

So we go back to the first chapter and our greatest needs. A man desires significance—and sexual activity helps him feel significant. A woman desires security—and the intimacy cultivated in a relationship brings security. It's out of the security of emotional and spiritual intimacy that women feel the freedom to express their sexuality.

So the paradox of the gospel applies because we have to deny ourselves and lay down our lives for our spouses in the area of sexuality.

The Big Idea

Physical intimacy is the by-product of many small sacrifices done with no ulterior motive.

Wives, sometimes you need to lead with sex and let the feelings of intimacy and security follow. Men, you need to cultivate a close relationship with your wife in the ordinary details of life, then let sex flow out naturally. Neither of you should demand or withhold sex as a way to manipulate your spouse and get your own way. Your marriage union means that your bodies actually belong to one another (1 Corinthians 7:1–5).

This paradox of the gospel is even woven into the sex act itself. Hopefully you have already experienced occasions where you were completely focused on pleasing your spouse during sex. And in the end you received much more pleasure in return. We give ourselves away sacrificially, we focus on the other person, their pleasure and their satisfaction, and, in the end we experience a deeper pleasure and satisfaction than we ever could have had any other way.

As you lower a candle snuffer over the wick of a candle, the smoke is trapped and replaces all the oxygen until finally the flame is extinguished. An atmosphere without oxygen extinguishes the flame.

When you look out for your own interests, you have the same effect in your marriage as a candle snuffer. When you focus on yourself, you create an atmosphere in your marriage that smothers the flame of passion.

Compare that to a butane lighter. That flame will keep burning indefinitely. Why? It's got a source of fuel constantly feeding the flame. When we make deposits into our spouse's emotional bank account, when we sacrifice for them, when we serve them, and when we love them the way they want to be loved, it adds fuel to the fire.

A (Slightly Disguised) True Story about...Sex
Brandon and Lauren (continued)

Early in their marriage, Brandon and Lauren made the choice to get involved in their church. They joined a small group. They served on ministry teams. They grew in their love for Christ.

After several years, Brandon and Lauren were finally able to talk to each other about some of their frustrations about sex. Lauren heard about some resources for dealing with abuse, and worked through several materials that helped her heal from the past.

Brandon learned to be patient and treasure Lauren's needs and pleasure more than his own. A lot of his dreams and fantasies died, but God gave him the wisdom to see that the only way to "fix" their sex life was to work through their problems one by one—there were no shortcuts. So as God changed his heart, he slowed down and helped Lauren walk forward one step at a time.

Since they understood they were in this together, they began to communicate more. They talked frankly about what worked and what didn't. They shared their frustrations and their fears.

Over the years, Lauren found herself enjoying sex more as the physical discomfort disappeared. Brandon began to experience the pleasure of focusing on the joy of his wife more than his own.

By the time they were married ten years, Brandon and Lauren were both very satisfied with the sexual aspect of their marriage. Brandon can recall thinking one special night, "Thank You, God, for allowing us to come this far."

You're right, we don't know your husband or your wife. But we know this: There is no Plan B. There is no alternative. There is no other way to do this.

You either:

look out for your own interest and do what the world says:
Try to make yourself happy, and get what you can,

OR

you deny yourself, you lay down your life for Christ,
and you serve your spouse.

Those are your only choices, and the Bible says only one of them leads to true happiness. Only one of those roads leads to truly great sex. Maybe not right away, maybe not in the short term, maybe not in five years, maybe not in ten years, maybe not in twenty years, but at some point you have to believe that you are going to find something greater than what you gave. That's the paradox of the gospel, that we lose our lives to find them again.

CHAPTER REVIEW

The following multiple choice questions review the concepts of this chapter. Choose the best answer based on what you learned..

1. A good acronym for maintaining sexual integrity is...

   a) WKRP

   b) NASA

   c) NFL

   d) ACT

2. The process of being drawn in by temptation was compared to...

   a) Custer at the Little Big Horn

   b) Anakin Skywalker in that scene where his face gets all angry

   c) a crab in a net

   d) how it feels when you get a paper cut right on the end of your little finger

3. There is a difference between men and women when it comes to...

   a) their taste in peanut butter

   b) their view of sex and intimacy

   c) shoe size

   d) the number of hairs in their eyebrows

4. When you look out for your own interests, in terms of sex you are being a...

   a) Greyhound bus

   b) candle snuffer

   c) greyhound dog

   d) stethoscope

You Haven't Finished This Chapter Until...

By now you know the drill. You could probably write this section. Hey, that's a good idea! If you were going to write to couples before they left this chapter on sex, what would you want to be sure to tell them?

_____

_____

_____

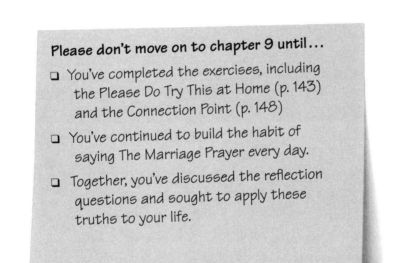

Please don't move on to chapter 9 until...

❑ You've completed the exercises, including the Please Do Try This at Home (p. 143) and the Connection Point (p. 148)

❑ You've continued to build the habit of saying The Marriage Prayer every day.

❑ Together, you've discussed the reflection questions and sought to apply these truths to your life.

Questions for Reflection and Discussion

1. How has your view of sex been affected by the culture? By your past circumstances? What difference has that made in your life?

2. Could you relate to anything in the "True Story" of this chapter? Why or why not? How could you apply some lesson from the story to your marriage?

3. Read the big idea again. Have you had the opportunity to sacrifice for your spouse with no ulterior motive? What did you learn?

4. Is there something you want to do differently because of what you read and talked about in this chapter? If so, what is it? How do you plan to change?

A One-Hour Deposit for the Heart
Section 4: Unity

As we've said, unity in your marriage won't come in one evening. But you can do things to enhance and maintain the sense of connection between you and your spouse. Here are a few practical ideas to make your prayer—"Make us one, like You are three in one"— a reality.

Plan an evening together around the house. If you have children, find some time to be alone, perhaps after the children go to bed. Consider including at least these three components in your time together.

1. **Go on a scavenger hunt.** The theme of your adventure is "unity." Each of you strike out on your own and take up to ten minutes to search your home for **three things** that represent some aspect of the unity in your marriage. Perhaps something that represents a shared interest, a picture of the family, a memento of a special trip, or a special gift. You may want to take a plastic bag with you to hide the items you find.

After you come back together, take turns revealing what you selected. Talk about why each one is special and what it represents.

2. **Touch your spouse.** Even if you already make a regular practice of expressing concern and affection, carve out some time to pay special attention to each other. Take a walk and hold hands. Sit close together on the couch and put your arm around your spouse. Give your spouse a foot or shoulder massage. Reconnect through the sense of touch, remembering that God has made you one flesh.

3. **Pray with one another.** Say The Marriage Prayer together. Pray also for personal needs and the rest of your family. Thank God for your spouse and the positive influence they are in your life. Ask God to continue to draw you closer to one another so that you would live out the reality of your prayer, "Make us one, like You are three in one."

Section 5: Attitude

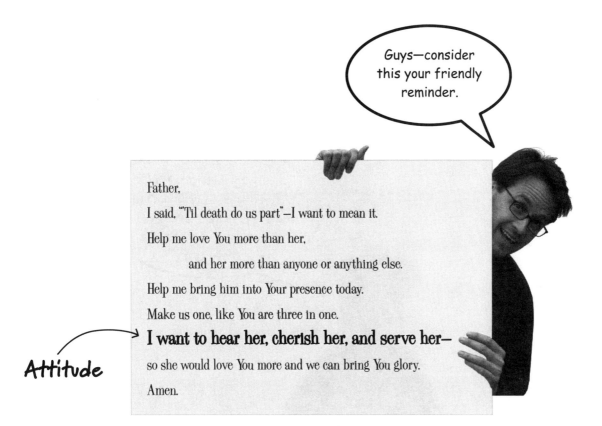

Guys—consider this your friendly reminder.

Father,

I said, "Til death do us part"—I want to mean it.

Help me love You more than her,

and her more than anyone or anything else.

Help me bring him into Your presence today.

Make us one, like You are three in one.

I want to hear her, cherish her, and serve her—

so she would love You more and we can bring You glory.

Amen.

Attitude

The next chapters are about our ATTITUDE. Most people today prize their independence. We don't like the thought that we have to depend on anyone else.

Yet, in marriage, the Bible says that you are no longer your own. You have been united to your spouse. You belong to each another.

In the next two chapters, we'll examine two big ideas:

- ► **Everyone is good at communicating about what is interesting to them.**
- ► **Most people live like money will do what it promises, and that God won't do what He promises.**

Both the way we communicate and the way we handle money reveal our attitudes toward our spouse, and toward God. Many couples have told us that these are two of the areas where they struggle. It's not easy to consistently love our spouse through the ups and downs of life. That's why we pray every day, "I want to hear him, support him, and serve him."

9: Communication

Valuing Your Spouse's Heart

Which of the following are the most important aspects of communication to you? (Pick three.)

Him:

- ❏ Honesty
- ❏ Tone of voice
- ❏ Brevity
- ❏ Other _____

- ❏ Good listening
- ❏ Gentleness
- ❏ Emotional connection

- ❏ Body language
- ❏ Calmness

Her:

- ❏ Honesty
- ❏ Tone of voice
- ❏ Brevity
- ❏ Other _____

- ❏ Good listening
- ❏ Gentleness
- ❏ Emotional connection

- ❏ Body language
- ❏ Calmness

Which of the following frustrate you the most when trying to communicate? (pick two)

Him:

- ❏ Repetition
- ❏ Tone of voice
- ❏ Lack of sincerity
- ❏ Other _____

- ❏ Loud voice
- ❏ Anger
- ❏ Dishonesty

- ❏ Body language
- ❏ Distractedness

Her:

- ❏ Repetition
- ❏ Tone of voice
- ❏ Lack of sincerity
- ❏ Other _____

- ❏ Loud voice
- ❏ Anger
- ❏ Dishonesty

- ❏ Body language
- ❏ Distractedness

RULES OF ENGAGEMENT

Discuss your answers with your spouse. What aspect of communication is most important to you? What's most frustrating?

A (Slightly Disguised) True Story about…Communication
Jamie and Chase

Jamie sat at the dining room table enjoying a few quiet moments and finishing her morning Bible reading. Things were much slower now with their empty nest. Chase, her husband, happened to be sitting at the other end of the table with a cup of coffee and his Bible.

Jamie glanced up and saw a delivery truck arrive at the house across the street. When she saw appliances being unloaded she remembered that her neighbors were remodeling their kitchen.

Over the next ten or so minutes, Jamie watched as new appliances were taken into the house and old appliances were removed. Occasionally, she made a comment to Chase: "Wow, look how big their new side-by-side refrigerator is" or "That new stove looks beautiful."

How would you have responded?

Jamie and Chase's kitchen is twenty-five years old. So after a few more minutes, Chase finished his coffee, got up, and as he walked by Jamie, said, "Honey, it's a sin to envy."

There was silence in the room.

To be continued…

Hopefully, by now you've been praying your Marriage Prayer every day for weeks. Is God using it to transform your attitudes and behavior in marriage? That's our prayer for you.

"I want to hear her, cherish her, and serve her." "I want to hear him, support him, and serve him." Why are these phrases in The Marriage Prayer? Because every person wants to be heard and to be loved. That's one of the greatest gifts we give to our spouses, and one of the things God uses to transform our hearts.

Whole books have been written about communication, and we get questions about it from men and women all the time.

Men and Communication

One of those common complaints we hear is that men are not good communicators. That's actually become an accepted mantra of married life. The wife wants to have a conversation; the guy wants to watch ESPN because he doesn't like to talk. But is this really true?

Take this one-question quiz: Men are good communicators.

❏ True
❏ False

Well, think about how communication happens in business. What does a person have to do at work to actually connect with another person and get work done? A man in business has to be clear; he has to be a good listener; he has to echo the thoughts of others and give feedback; he has to respond in a timely manner; he has to make eye contact; and he has to have positive body language.

Sounds like the ingredients of good communication to us.

So, are men good communicators? It depends. They can be when they want to be.

The **BIG** Idea:

Everyone is good at communicating about what is interesting to them.

Pat's younger brother, Bill, is not much of a talker. He's the baby in the family. Pat has another brother, Pete, who is much more communicative. Over the years Bill has become a very quiet person. Basically, he decided he didn't want to fight for airtime.

However, a few years ago Bill became interested in flying small planes. He bought a little Piper Cub and flew all the way from Florida to California. Now whenever the family gets together Bill talks nonstop about his plane and his travels.

Everybody is a good communicator about what is interesting to them.

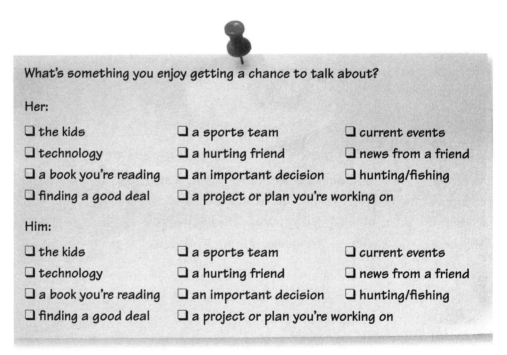

What's something you enjoy getting a chance to talk about?

Her:

❑ the kids   ❑ a sports team   ❑ current events
❑ technology   ❑ a hurting friend   ❑ news from a friend
❑ a book you're reading ❑ an important decision   ❑ hunting/fishing
❑ finding a good deal   ❑ a project or plan you're working on

Him:

❑ the kids   ❑ a sports team   ❑ current events
❑ technology   ❑ a hurting friend   ❑ news from a friend
❑ a book you're reading ❑ an important decision   ❑ hunting/fishing
❑ finding a good deal   ❑ a project or plan you're working on

Communicating Well

The Bible actually says quite a bit about what makes communication work.

My dear brothers, take note of this: Everyone should be quick to listen, slow to speak and slow to become angry. (James 1:19)

Listen first; take your time before speaking; don't fly off the handle.

Kings take pleasure in honest lips; they value a man who speaks the truth. (Proverbs 16:13)

Honesty really is the best policy.

Do you see a man who speaks in haste? There is more hope for a fool than for him. (Proverbs 29:20)

Don't ever say the first thing that comes to your mind, unless it's the second thing also.

The good man brings good things out of the good stored up in his heart, and the evil man brings evil things out of the evil stored up in his heart. For out of the overflow of his heart his mouth speaks. (Luke 6:45)

The words you say reflect the attitudes and beliefs of your heart—change the heart, change the words.

Of course, in a fallen world we are never going to have perfect communication. And so a lack of communication often leads to misunderstanding. But unfortunately, so does communication. No matter how much you say, there are always things left unsaid and areas of interpretation. Communicating well is hard work.

Communication and the Heart

Communicating well is also incredibly important. How we communicate reveals the reality of what's in our hearts. If you lose your temper when speaking to your boss, your spouse, or a friend—you'll have bad communication. But those people are not creating your anger, they are only revealing it. "Out of the overflow of his heart his mouth speaks."

Communication is one of the primary tools God has given for impacting the lives of others. If you and your spouse are to live as "one flesh" like you've been praying in The Marriage Prayer, you have to communicate well. God uses communication to transform lives.

> *A man finds joy in giving an apt reply—and how good is a timely word!* (Proverbs 15:23)

> *A wise man's heart guides his mouth, and his lips promote instruction. Pleasant words are a honeycomb, sweet to the soul and healing to the bones.* (Proverbs 16:23–24)

That sounds great—I'd love to communicate like this in my marriage. But what do you suggest we ACTUALLY DO?

We're so glad you asked! Here are our top five practical ideas to help improve your communication.

Five Do's and Don'ts

1   Don't Underestimate
Your Differences   ⟶   **Instead**   ⟶   Celebrate Who God
Has Made You to Be

A few years ago we had our Man in the Mirror faculty from around the country fly into Orlando for a conference. That year we decided to race go-carts for team building. On Monday night there was a dinner, and Pat made the mistake of letting some of the guys know that he intended to lap everybody at least once. Needless to say, word got around. The next day, instead of go-carts, it was bumper cars. Even the most mild-mannered of our faculty came out and attacked Pat with the cunning of a coyote. It was unbelievable. Blocking motions, ramming motions, spinning him out. Pat had bone bruises and shattered the PDA he had mistakenly left in his pocket. He never knew who to blame because he had six different guys claiming the credit.

Contrast that with Pat's experience a couple of weeks before. He had gone down to the track to check it out, and there were several high school girls driving on the course. Pat was anxious to see how fast the go-carts could move, but one of the girls was driving slowly in front of him and would not move out of his way. So Pat began to gently nudge and bump her cart to let her know she needed to speed up or get out of the way. Finally, she said, "Okay, well go ahead then."

Everybody knows that men and women are different. In communication, the differences are a lot like the differences on a go-cart track.

Men want to get around the track as fast as possible. Their goal is to get to the finish line and accomplish what they started.

Not to overly stereotype this, but women are typically not as concerned about going fast. They are interested in the journey.

Here's a great question to demonstrate the difference in communication between men and women.

Pop Quiz

How did you feel the last time you had to tell someone something and they interrupted you and said they already knew what you were going to say? (Take three minutes to discuss your answer.)

Most men who answer this question would say that they felt nothing or were relieved. If a man thinks he is going to have to go into a lot of detail to give an update on a project to a colleague, then finds the colleague has already been updated by someone else, he is basically glad that the information was transferred without him having to do it.

Most women would have a different reaction, to say the least.

Most men communicate to transfer information, while women communicate to connect emotionally. Of course this is not always the case, but it tends to be true as a general rule.

Much of the time that a man is communicating with a woman, he is trying to pass along information. He's operating from a base of reason. There is something he is trying to accomplish and communicating with his wife is part of that process.

For most women, the process is just as important as the result. Why would a wife repeat the same question several times over period of hours?

Wife: "Do you think it's okay for Billy to spend the night at Jay's house?"

Husband: "Sure."

              An hour later.

Wife: "Honey, are you sure it's okay for Billy to spend the night at Jay's house?"

Husband: "Yes, honey, it's okay."

              A few hours later.

Wife: "Should we really let Billy spend the night at Jay's house?"

Husband: "How many times do we have to talk about this? Let him go, HE'S EIGHTEEN YEARS OLD."

A woman is not only interested in an answer to her question; she desires reassurance. She wants to be listened to, to be heard, and to be understood.

Husbands, don't shut down your wife's opportunity to unburden her heart in communication. A woman has emotional tension that builds in her heart, and the way she discharges that emotional tension is by expressing feelings through communication. So let her express her thought.

Wives, don't take it too personally if you want to have a deep meaningful conversation about alternative paint colors for the kitchen and your husband keeps glancing at *SportsCenter*. Respect the fact that he sees communication as a task, and help him see the end result you are trying to achieve.[1]

---

1. Want to understand more about the differences between men and women? Check out Paul Tournier's classic book, *To Understand Each Other*. Also, Pat's book *Devotions for Couples* has a whole section with two-page chapters to help improve communication.

2 Don't Dismiss Your ⟶ **Instead** ⟶ Substitute Discipline for a
Spouse's Interests   Lack of Natural Interest

Imagine you're a guy headed to a business appointment with a woman from another company. You begin by talking about your company, and then she talks about her company. But you want to go deeper. You say, "What do you do in your spare time?" And she says, "Well, I love the ballet." And you're thinking, "What?" But you say, "That's fascinating, tell me more." So she takes that as a signal that you're really interested and launches into a fifteen-minute explanation of all the intricacies of ballet history. You're doing everything you can to keep your eyelids from closing. You have to keep them open to save the deal!

How does this apply to marriage? One of the most crucial things to do in communication is to not dismiss your spouse's interests. They are going to like different things than you. That's okay—it just means you have to manage these differences.

Pat loves to spend time with his wife, Patsy. The problem is that most of the things that Pat likes, Patsy doesn't like, and most of the things that she likes, he doesn't like. So they have had to work hard to not put unfair expectations and demands on each other. You can't expect people to respond with immediate enthusiasm about things they are not naturally interested in.

You can, however, expect to be treated at least with loving courtesy. So you need to make an effort to explore your spouse's interests. See if they are doing something where you can join in.

When Pat got a Harley-Davidson a few years ago, he had some highway pegs added for his feet to make it easier to take long rides. He was excited about the upgrade to his bike so he told Patsy all about it. He finally said, "Come on out in the garage. Let me show you." You know what she did? She said, "Great, let's do it!" So she, with great enthusiasm, went out to the garage to Pat's motorcycle. She scored some serious points.

3   Don't Consult ——————▶   **Instead** ——————▶   **Console**
         (or Counsel)

Everyone has burdens, and everyone is looking for someone to share them with. That's one of the roles we need to play for our spouses.

But when our spouse shares a burden or concern, we need to learn to be a consoler, not a consultant. We need to listen without feeling the need to give advice or solve their problem.

People dread receiving advice. What happens when you get unwanted advice? If you're like most people, you begin to shut down. If you get unwanted advice repetitively, then you won't share the burdens of your heart. That puts a pretty big crimp in a marriage.

Instead of giving advice, listen quietly and console. Nod your head. Send a message with your eyes. Your body language can say that you love this person unconditionally, you accept them, and you want to be the person with whom they can share their burdens.

A (Slightly Disguised) True Story about...Communication
Jamie and Chase (continued)

That's wise! No anger, no withdrawal.

Jamie chose not to respond immediately to Chase's comment. Ironically, Jamie continued reading her Bible that morning and came to, "Love must be sincere" (Romans 12:9). While Chase's approach may not have been perfect, she believed he was acting in honesty and love. After all, nobody knew her like he did.

God definitely wanted to teach her something.

A few days later, she read Romans 13:9: "The commandments, 'Do not commit adultery,' 'Do not murder,' 'Do not steal,' 'Do not covet,' and whatever other commandment there may be, are summed up in this one rule: 'Love your neighbor as yourself.'"

Jamie felt convicted by the Holy Spirit. Later that week she came to the verse, "Rather, clothe yourselves with the Lord Jesus Christ,

and do not think about how to gratify the desires of the sinful nature"
(Romans 13:14).

   *She prayed and decided that instead of envy, she would thank God
for His many blessings.*

To be continued…

---

4   Don't Respond to Conflict with Anger or Withdrawal   →   **Instead**   →   Develop the Habit of Being Completely Frank with Each Other

Conflict is such an important topic we covered it in detail in Chapter 3. But here we want to help you communicate through conflict.

Connection Point

How much honesty is there in your communication today compared to five years ago?

Him:

Much Less Honesty	Less Honesty	More Honesty	Much More Honesty

Her:

Much Less Honesty	Less Honesty	More Honesty	Much More Honesty

There are at least two dysfunctional responses to conflict. One is anger, and one is withdrawal. Some people get into a conflict and want to lash out with angry words. Others feel a conflict coming on and begin to withdraw from the relationship. Notice that both of these responses are absolutely destined to fail in terms of really working through the conflict. Anger can make your partner back down, and withdrawal can lead to pretending there was no conflict, but neither response can actually move your relationship forward.

What can help you get beyond a conflict? As we mentioned earlier, one thing successful couples do is develop the patience and commitment to be completely frank with each other. Sometimes emotions run hot. In that case, it would be better to say, "You know we really do need to deal with this constructively. I'm more angry than I should be right now, so why don't we have a cooling-off period? Then maybe, after dinner tonight, we could sit down and talk this through."

Paul Tournier says, "A lack of complete frankness is the greatest problem in communication." Over a period of years, certain areas can become off limits because you know how your spouse will respond if you bring up this particular issue. So, whole aspects of your relationship fall into a state of disrepair. That creates a dysfunctional relationship because you don't have the honesty and the frankness to deal with these issues. That's why the Scriptures place so much value on "honest lips."

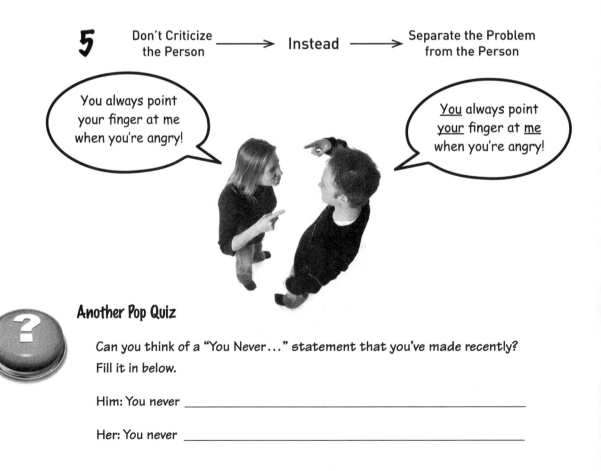

Another Pop Quiz

Can you think of a "You Never…" statement that you've made recently? Fill it in below.

Him: You never _____

Her: You never _____

Can you think of a "You Always" statement that you've made recently? Fill it in below.

Him: You always _____

Her: You always _____

So what do you do when your spouse irritates you or makes you angry? Don't criticize the person.

Criticism is a communication killer. When you criticize your spouse, they will be on the defensive and you will enter a downward spiral.

Yet we just said to be honest about how you feel. So how do you do that without criticizing your spouse?

The key is to separate the issue from the person. Don't attack your spouse personally; instead talk about the issue that is causing the conflict in a way that doesn't accuse or criticize.

One easy way to do this is to avoid "you" statements. These always come off as criticism. "You" don't keep a very clean house. "You" drive too fast. "You" don't discipline the children properly.

Instead, make statements that express how you feel about the situation. Say, "When the house is dirty, it makes me feel discouraged and uncomfortable." It lowers the temperature of your conversation. Instead of saying, "You work too much," say, "I feel frustrated when the kids and I don't know whether you will make it home before bedtime."

NBAS (No-Brainer Action Step)

Convert the following "you" statement into an "I feel" statement: "You always interrupt me when I am trying to talk to you."

---◆---

A (Slightly Disguised) True Story about…Communication
Jamie and Chase (continued)

Frankness! and
"I feel…"

That night Jamie told Chase what had happened during the week in her Bible study. Chase shared frankly how her comments about the neighbor's kitchen made him feel inadequate as a provider. He felt like she wasn't appreciating what they did have and the choices they had made together.

They talked about their decision years ago to provide a memorable family vacation every year for their entire family. They both realized that if they had cut out a few of those vacations they could have paid for a new kitchen. But which of the vacation memories would they have given up? The one where their son Josh learned to boogie board for the first time? The week when their oldest daughter got to go to town with the ladies for her first girls' day out?

God used Chase
to help open
Jamie's heart so
she could love Him
and her neighbor.
God gets the
glory!

They apologized to one another and were so grateful to have the opportunity to get back on the same page.

One morning the neighbors drove by when Jamie was working in the yard. They stopped and rolled down the window. Jamie stood up and said, "How are you all doing?"

"We're doing great. I'm hanging pictures in our new kitchen—you'll have to come over and inspect the finished product."

"I'd love to. But I don't want to inspect, I just want to share in your blessings."

These five ideas about communication have the potential to make a tremendous impact on your marriage.

* Don't Underestimate Your Differences—
Instead, Celebrate Who God Has Made You to Be

* **Don't Dismiss Your Spouse's Interests—**
  Instead, Substitue Discipline for a Lack of Natual Interest.

* **Don't Consult (or Counsel)—**
  Instead, Console

* **Don't Respond to Conflict with Anger or Withdrawal—**
  Instead, Develop the Habit of Being Completely Frank with Each Other

* **Don't Criticize the Person**
  Instead, Separate the Problem from the Person

Here's a case in point: A friend of ours was working too hard a few years ago. He called home one afternoon and told his wife, "Honey, I'm sorry, but I'm going to have to take an emergency trip and be out of town for three nights."

"That's okay," she said. "It's really easier when you're gone. At least then I don't have to worry about answering the kids about what time you're actually going to be home." She said this without rancor.

Her honesty was a wake-up call. Instead of getting angry about what she said or withdrawing, he started an honest dialogue with his wife, with more than a few tears. He now looks back on this as an episode that God used to save his marriage.

Why is communicating well a big deal? It's not just so you can have a happy marriage and avoid conflict. The answer is right there in the prayer you've been saying every day.

> **I want to hear her, cherish her, and serve her—**
> **so she would love You more and we can bring You glory.**

Communication is one of the tools we have to help shape our spouse's heart. God uses our words and body language to create an environment to draw our spouse to Himself. Our communication is for us, but even more so, it's a means for God to work in and through us for His glory.

Who doesn't want to end his days in a rocking chair next to a person who has become a passionate, mature disciple of Jesus Christ? If you communicate well, you can get there from here. Do it today—for your spouse and for the glory of God.

CHAPTER REVIEW

Find fourteen key concepts from this chapter hidden in the puzzle below (the answer key is on page 215)…

Don'ts		Do's	
ANGER	CONSULT	CLARITY	CONSOLE
COUNSEL	CRITICIZE	FRANKNESS	GENTLENESS
DEFEND	WITHDRAWAL	HONESTY	I FEEL
YOUSTATEMENTS		LISTEN	

```
Y  T  S  E  N  O  H  D  Q  C  R  L  S
S  S  E  N  E  L  T  N  E  G  E  E  Q
E  Z  I  C  I  T  I  R  C  C  G  S  P
C  O  N  S  O  L  E  L  E  O  N  N  S
C  L  A  R  I  T  Y  F  I  N  A  U  N
S  T  N  E  M  E  T  A  T  S  U  O  Y
D  N  E  F  E  D  N  Q  W  U  T  C  S
I  F  E  E  L  X  Q  K  O  L  C  E  E
F  R  A  N  K  N  E  S  S  T  B  X  N
W  I  T  H  D  R  A  W  A  L  D  X  O
```

You Haven't Finished This Chapter Until…

Remember, there are plenty of good marriage books that you can just read and forget. We didn't go to all this effort for this to be another one. We prayerfully expect that God will use this chapter to change your marriage. But that probably means you have to do something!

So, don't go on to the next chapter until...

☐ You've done all the exercises, including the Connection Point (p. 171) and the No-Brainer Action Step (p. 173).

☐ You are continuing the habit of praying The Marriage Prayer every day.

☐ Together, you've discussed the reflection questions and asked how these truths might apply to your life.

Questions for Reflection and Discussion

Use the questions to cement the ideas from this chapter into your heart and marriage. Discuss them with your spouse and your small group of couples.

1. If communication is so important in marriage, why do you think it can be so difficult?

2. What parts of the "True Story" in this chapter could you relate to? What aspects seemed foreign to you? What lessons could you learn from it for your marriage?

3. Which of the five suggestions in this chapter will be most important to your marriage? Why?

4. What is one practical take-away you garnered from this chapter that you will implement in the next week? How will you do it?

10: Money
Treasuring Your Spouse's Heart

Are you and your wife on the same page when it comes to money? Here's a quick exercise to kick off your discussion.

Rate **yourself** on the following money scales. Circle the number which best represents your agreement on these statements. Strongly Disagree is 1; Strongly Agree is 10.

1

I like to save and invest.

Him	1	2	3	4	5	6	7	8	9	10
Her	1	2	3	4	5	6	7	8	9	10

2

I like to have nice things.

Him	1	2	3	4	5	6	7	8	9	10
Her	1	2	3	4	5	6	7	8	9	10

3

I like to give money away.

Him	1	2	3	4	5	6	7	8	9	10
Her	1	2	3	4	5	6	7	8	9	10

4

I love to find bargains and make smart purchases.

Him	1	2	3	4	5	6	7	8	9	10
Her	1	2	3	4	5	6	7	8	9	10

RULES OF ENGAGEMENT

Discuss your ratings. Would you have rated your spouse the same way they did? Did anything surprise you about your answers? Why or why not?

A (Slightly Disguised) True Story about... Money
Jason and Rachel

"Are you sure you want to do this?" Rachel sat in front of the computer with bills stacked beside her.

Jason plopped down into a chair across the room. "Honey, we talked this through. We agreed it's not the best answer, but this is important."

"You're right. Let's go ahead and do it." Even though they didn't have the money, Rachel clicked the mouse to order the tickets for their trip to the Caribbean.

When Jason and Rachel got married, they didn't have a clue about how to manage money. Jason grew up in a family that didn't have any money to manage. Rachel's mom and dad had been divorced multiple times—lessons about money were not the highest priority.

They both came into marriage with debt. Even with well-paying jobs, as fast as the money came in it went back out again. They didn't spend it on anything big, but between meals, clothes, entertainment, and a few items for the house, their debt continued to grow and grow. They eventually owed 20 percent of their annual income on credit cards.

Now, married almost ten years, making a nice income but still loaded with debt, they wanted to take a special trip to celebrate their tenth anniversary. So they charged the tickets to their credit card.

To be continued...

What was the last tough choice you had to make about money?

In research, problems with money are one of the strongest and most consistent predictors of eventual divorce. When a person felt their spouse spent money foolishly, the odds of eventual divorce more than doubled.[1] This was shown to be true for both men and women.[2]

We have more choices for how to use money today than any society in history—leisure activities, travel, hobbies, electronics, furniture, investing, charities, events, insurance, and on and on. No wonder it's so easy for us to have disagreements with our spouse.

Let's get this straight: **Money is very important**. When the 10th of the month rolls around, the mortgage company isn't looking for Jesus. They want cash.

What Is Money, Anyway?

Not only is money important; it's also a friend of the family. There's nothing evil about money. If you have money, you know it's a blessing to be able to have an orderly house. If you don't have money, you know what a curse it is to be in financial chaos.

Money is a tool that God has given to help you do what He has called you to do. But it's also so much more than that. It's a sacred trust. It's something God has given you to steward for His glory.

Money is also very risky. Consider the following Scriptures:

> *For the love of money is a root of all kinds of evil.* (1 Timothy 6:10)

> *What does it profit a man to gain the whole world, and forfeit his soul?* (Mark 8:36 NASB)

> *Watch out! Be on your guard against all kinds of greed; a man's life does not consist in the abundance of his possessions.* (Luke 12:15)

Money is so dangerous because it makes promises that it cannot keep.

---

1. P. R. Amato and S. J. Rogers, "A Longitudinal Study of Marital Problems and Subsequent Divorce," *Journal of Marriage and the Family*, 59 (1997): 612–624.

2. T. Terling-Watt, "Explaining Divorce: An Examination of the Relationship Between Marital Characteristics and Divorce," *Journal of Divorce and Remarriage*, 35# (2001): 125–145.

Like a lot of young couples, when David and Ruthie got married, they furnished their apartment with whatever they could find. Their sofa was a hand-me-down. Their bookshelf was two wood slats resting on four cement blocks.

The brown recliner in the corner was already old by the time it had arrived in the dorm room of David's older brother. Then it had a few neglectful years in David's college room. Finally, it had come to rest in David and Ruthie's apartment.

After a few years of marriage, Ruthie became pregnant. When the time came for the baby to be born, David and Ruthie decided they wanted a rocking chair for the baby— and David. The plan was to replace the sagging, brown recliner with one that rocked.

David still remembers coming home after work the day it arrived. As he sat in the new chair, it was almost as if money was talking to him inside his head.

David's super sweet circa 1990 mauve overstuffed recliner.

Money:	You made a great choice with this recliner.
David:	Thanks.
Money:	Yeah, I love the way it rocks and reclines.
David:	It swivels too!
Money:	That's cool! Why don't you close your eyes and enjoy it?
David:	Okay.
Money:	(after a minute of silence) Hey—open your eyes.
David:	Yeah?
Money:	Now that you've got a great recliner, don't you think we ought to do something about that grungy sofa?

It took only five minutes after their major purchase to start thinking about the next thing he needed.

Yes, money talks. It says, "I can make you happy by giving you the desires of your heart." But that's a lie. The Bible puts it this way: "Whoever loves money never has money enough; whoever loves wealth is never satisfied with his income" (Ecclesiastes 5:10).

How We Got Where We Are

We live in the most affluent culture in the history of the world. Things we take for granted—refrigerators, air conditioning, televisions, cable or satellite, computers, automobiles, telephones—were not part of the average person's life just one hundred years ago. They still aren't in many parts of the world.

Since we've added these things to our basic standard of living, we've also added the pressure of paying for them. Do the math—you'll find over half your expenses go for things almost no one had one hundred years ago.

Our society has been shaped by four powerful economic forces.

1. Mass Production—Henry Ford started a revolution. His ideas about assembly lines and replaceable parts allowed businesses to produce products and gadgets at prices low enough to make them affordable to the average household.

2. Mass Communication—Late in the nineteenth century, the rise of newspapers, radio, and magazines ushered in an era that gave people all across the country access to the same information. In the twentieth century, live television meant we were watching the same images in real time. And now in the twenty-first century, the Internet connects us to information from all over the world at the click of a computer mouse.

3. Mass Marketing—Companies use this means of communication to create markets for the new products they were able to make. They convince us how much better our lives will be with their product or service. Who knew they needed a food dehydrator before late-night infomercials?

4. Installment Credit—There's a limit to how many products people can buy with money they've already earned, so companies developed ways for them to be able to purchase products **now** by "pledging" money they will earn **later**. In the 1950s, Diner's Club and American Express introduced the first general purpose credit cards.

Guys, uhmm, I don't want to make you feel bad, but this is a marriage book, remember?

Yeah, we remember. Believe it or not, this is really important.

Three Resulting Attitudes

These four forces have had a profound impact on the thinking of the average person, including the average married couple.

first attitude — People have moved from a culture of production to a **culture of consumption**. Just 150 years ago most people would have identified themselves by what they produced—whether a farmer, store owner, or blacksmith. Today, most people see their work as simply a way to get resources to consume items they need and want. We used to work as an end in itself; now we work as a means to buy things.

second attitude — Things we want are so readily accessible, reasonably priced, beautifully marketed, and attractively financed "with easy monthly payments." We don't need to be patient and wait until we can actually afford them! We can practice **immediate gratification**.

third attitude — Companies have produced some amazing stuff. Who doesn't want the latest computer, camera, or cell phone? Their marketing hype that things will bring happiness and satisfaction is both alluring and seductive. It's easy to develop a **"gotta-have-it" focus**, looking for the next thing we can acquire.

These three attitudes profoundly affect the way we deal with our money.

A (Slightly Disguised) True Story about…Money
Jason and Rachel (continued)

After getting married, Jason and Rachel had become active in church. They worked with the middle-school youth group and spent time with other young couples. They joined an adult class on Sundays and learned more about the Bible.

Jason did well at his work, and Rachel took a variety of jobs to bring in some extra income. As their income grew, the issue of debt became less and less of a worry. But it was always there in the back of their minds.

Over the next few years God began to change their view of money. They learned the importance of giving to their church. Things they would have purchased without thought now brought pause. When they tried to buy their first house, they wondered why they hadn't saved more for the down payment. Eventually, by the time they had been married a decade, they were consciously trying to avoid more debt and get rid of the debt they had. Their tenth anniversary trip was the last major purchase they financed with their credit cards.

Finally, after they had been married thirteen years, they decided to make a plan and work the plan. They would get out of debt once and for all.

To be continued…

How has God changed your view of money?

Four Lifestyle Choices

There are four lifestyles from which we will choose. Pat has written about these in more detail, but we want to provide an overview here.

1. "Above" their means. People who live above their means have chosen to spend more than they make. Every month they are getting deeper and deeper in debt. For whatever reason, they cannot seem to control their spending. They are living in a house of cards, and it will eventually come tumbling down.

2. "At" their means. This couple spends everything that comes in. They aren't digging a deeper hole, but neither are they saving for a rainy day. They don't have a retirement plan, they don't tithe, they don't have life insurance. Everything they earn goes to fund their current lifestyle.

3. "Within" their means. This couple understands that they are stewards of all that God has given them. So they are strategic with their money. They have good insurance for illness or death. They have a retirement plan so they can still do the things God calls them to do in their later years. They are generous toward the kingdom of God—they give at least 10 percent of their income first. As a result of these things, they experience a great sense of contentment.

4. "Below" their means. This couple has the gift of giving. They have intentionally decided to live on less than their total income. They live in a house smaller than one they could afford, and drive a less-expensive car than their peers. They give the money they would have spent on more things to Christ's work. They're having an impact all out of proportion to what they might ordinarily do; and they have the joy that comes with it.

 **Connection Point**

Independently rate your marriage on the following scale.

Him:
|——————————————————————————————————|
below   within   at   above
your means   your means   your means your means

Her:
|——————————————————————————————————|
below   within   at   above
your means   your means   your means your means

Do you agree on where you are? If not, talk about why you have a different opinion.

Do you want a lifestyle that's different than the one you have? How would you go about changing your lifestyle? In the end you have to be more committed to God than you are to money. "No one can serve two masters. Either he will hate the one and love the other, or he will be devoted to the one and despise the other. You cannot serve both God and Money." (Matthew 6:24). So it has to come from the heart first—God has to change you from the inside out.

The Big Idea

Most people live like money <u>will do</u> what it promises and that God <u>won't do</u> what He promises.

Money used rightly is a great blessing. Money running amuck will make a huge mess of your life. Ask God to help you put money in its place.

Money Matters in Marriage

In 2000, there were 56 million Americans aged 55 and older. Among those, 32 percent were widowed women but only 9 percent were widowed men. Men, it's more than three times more likely that your wife will outlive you. Don't neglect providing for your wife!

A few years ago Pat was going through his mom's papers after her death. One sheet was from the Social Security Administration. His mother died on May 1, and she had received $2,390 for those four months of income—about $7,000 annualized. (Pat's dad had received about $13,000 in the same year.) That's not a lot of money for two elderly people to live on.

A good start would be for the two of you to come to an agreement on the major priorities for money. The next two pages list seven key priorities. Please place a ✓ in the box beside the ones where you feel like you are doing well. Place an X beside the ones you feel needs some attention.

Him: ❑
Her: ❑
Get on the same page about the purpose of money. Money can be a source of conflict if you don't agree on where it comes from and what it's for. "The blessing of the Lord brings wealth, and he adds no trouble to it" (Proverbs 10:22). Financial blessing comes from God. Use this chapter to discuss your views and come to agreement about your finances.

Him: ❑
Her: ❑
Use money to accomplish what God has called you to do. Money is a tool God has given to empower you to do things He's called you to do. What are your primary callings and responsibilities? Take care of your children, invest in the kingdom through your church, find an avenue for personal ministry, impact the people in your neighborhood, and help friends in the workplace—use your money to pursue your callings with passion.

Him: ❑
Her: ❑
Earn and save money slowly but surely. "Dishonest money dwindles away, but he who gathers money little by little makes it grow" (Proverbs 13:11). Don't go after "get rich quick" schemes. Be sensible and provide for both now and the future.

Him: ❑
Her: ❑
Save for retirement according to a plan. "In the house of the wise are stores of choice food and oil, but a foolish man devours all he has" (Proverbs 21:20). Don't depend on the government or others to support you in your elderly years. Put some of your resources aside for the future when you may no longer be able to earn them. Consider getting a professional to help you make a plan.

Him: ❑
Her: ❑
Don't let money become an idol. It's easy to depend on money to provide security. But you can never have enough money to protect against all the risks in the world. "Command those who are rich in this present world not to be arrogant nor to put their hope in wealth, which is so uncertain, but to put their hope in God, who richly provides us with everything for our enjoyment" (1 Timothy 6:17).

Him: ❏   **Don't get in debt; and if you're in debt, get out.** Debt is dumb. Common
Her: ❏   sense tells you that it takes more energy to earn a living **and** pay off debts
than it takes to just earn a living. The Bible affirms this.

Him: ❏   **Make choices that relieve pressure, not add to it.** Do you habitually make
Her: ❏   bad and impulsive choices? Don't buy things you can't afford. Make a
budget and stick to it. "Be sure you know the condition of your flocks; and
give careful attention to your herds for riches do not endure forever" (Proverbs
27:23–24). Think like a steward!

> My son, if you have put up security for your neighbor, if you have struck
> hands in pledge for another… then do this, my son, to free yourself, since
> you have fallen into your neighbor's hands: Go and humble yourself; press
> your plea with your neighbor! Allow no sleep to your eyes, no slumber to your
> eyelids. Free yourself, like a gazelle from the hand of the hunter, like a bird
> from the snare of the fowler. (Proverbs 6:1, 3–5)

> Do not be a man who strikes hands in pledge or puts up security for debts;
> if you lack the means to pay, your very bed will be snatched from under you.
> (Proverbs 22:26–27)

In his business life, Pat Morley eventually decided to pretend those verses weren't
there. He looked for a loophole because he had to borrow money as a real estate devel-
oper. At first he said, "I'm not going to personally guarantee a loan." He would only
borrow if the property itself was the sole collateral. Then the perfect deal came along,
and he made the decision that he would sign personally—"just this once."

After that he signed regularly. Once you've kicked sand to cover the line that you've
drawn, it's very easy to violate your principles over and over again.

He spent seven years signing personally for loans. After he decided to obey the Bible,
it took another seven years for him to get out of debt.

Some people reading this book will assume they are smarter than Pat. You may be
thinking, "That will never happen to me." That's what Pat thought too!

Our advice? Don't ruin what otherwise could be the best years of your life. Get out of
debt as fast as you can.

Him: ❏   **Enjoy your money.** One of the reasons God gives us money is to enjoy His
Her: ❏   good gifts. Use your resources to make memories. Invest it in fun experiences with family and friends. Don't hoard your money so much that your spouse doesn't have enough to live. If you are squeezing your money so hard that George Washington is turning red, live a little. Have fun with what God has provided.

Him: ❏   **Give it away.** Once you get in the habit, there is almost nothing more fun to
Her: ❏   do with money than to give it away. "Sell your possessions and give to the poor. Provide purses for yourselves that will not wear out, a treasure in heaven that will not be exhausted, where no thief comes near and no moth destroys. For where your treasure is, there your heart will be also" (Luke 12:33–34). As the cliché says, you can't take it with you, but you can send it on ahead.

PLEASE DO TRY THIS AT HOME

Which of the major money issues did you check as doing well? Which ones did you mark as needing some attention?

A (Slightly Disguised) True Story about...Money
Jason and Rachel (continued)

The summer when their oldest child was nine, Jason and Rachel decided to become completely free of consumer debt in the next year. Instead of an expensive family vacation, they chose a less-expensive option at a nearby beach.

They took all their financial information with them. They finalized a plan, then sat down with their children and talked about the changes they were going to make. They told them they would not be eating out at restaurants like in the past. Birthdays and Christmas would be a little different this year. They shared why they thought it was important to do this as a family.

They look back at that trip as perhaps their best vacation ever. Within a year Jason and Rachel had paid off all their credit card debt.

Now a few more years have gone by, and Jason and Rachel would tell you they haven't arrived in terms of dealing with money. Their children are teenagers now and the struggles are different—mainly how to best use the financial blessings that God has provided. But now they actively pray and ask God what He wants them to do. One of the things they are most excited about? By God's grace they feel they are giving their children a legacy they never received—a biblical view of money.

Money is a tool to accomplish God's calling.

Do you know Sally? You've been going to the little diner where she works for about three years. Her tables are on the other side of the diner from where you always sit. She's about seventy. Being a waitress is a noble vocation, but you just have the sense that this is not her natural place. You suspect that her life circumstances were different; she hasn't always been a waitress.

One day the question comes to you, "I wonder what Sally is doing working in this diner? Why isn't she with her grandchildren?" She's working there because she and her husband didn't provide for themselves financially.

Is it right for either you or your spouse to spend so much today that your family would be forced to abandon that lifestyle if you die or become disabled?

Pat had a friend who died suddenly. Several times in the last few years of his life he had his wife sign papers. It turned out she was cosigning unsecured notes totaling $60,000. Of course she's sad that he's gone, but she's also angry with him. How could he do that to her? Pat's angry, too. Pat told her, "When we get to heaven, I'm going to hold him down, then you spank him. And, when you get tired, you hold him because I want to spank him, too."

Don't let the blessing of God become a curse. Get on the same page and use your money for the glory of God.

CHAPTER REVIEW

As we told you in chapter 4, an anagram is the rearrangement of the letters in one word to spell another word or words. Like "Dormitory" and "Dirty Room." Unscramble the anagrams of important words from this chapter. We've completed the first one for you as an example. (If you need it, the answer key is on page 215.)

Anagram		Key Word from Chapter
candour is stomp	=	mass production
direct	=	_____
great mink	=	_____
invent stem	=	_____
entire term	=	_____
semipros	=	_____

You Haven't Finished This Chapter Until...

You've done this enough times now that you know what we are trying to do. We want you to take a deep breath and allow God to really work however He wants to work. Don't just let this be another chapter you check off the list. What does He want to teach you about money?

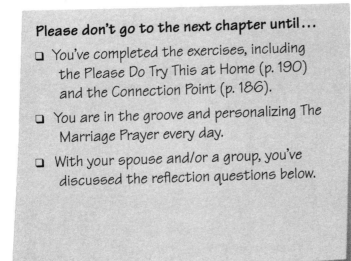

Please don't go to the next chapter until...

☐ You've completed the exercises, including
the Please Do Try This at Home (p. 190)
and the Connection Point (p. 186).

☐ You are in the groove and personalizing The
Marriage Prayer every day.

☐ With your spouse and/or a group, you've
discussed the reflection questions below.

Questions for Reflection and Discussion

1. What forces have most shaped your view of money? How has that impacted
your marriage?

2. Which parts of the "True Story" connect with your experience? How could
you apply some lesson from the story to your life?

3. Read the big idea again. When do you feel the temptation to trust money
more than God? How do you think you can get beyond that?

4. What application step sticks out at you from this chapter? How do you
plan to implement it?

A One-Hour Deposit for the Heart

Section 5: Attitude

Here's a deposit you can make in the heart of your spouse to demonstrate the attitude you want to have in your marriage. This is an opportunity to make your prayer—"I want to hear him, support him, and serve him"—a reality.

1. Look at your schedules and find a free hour when you could be together. Pick a place to meet—in your home, at a quiet restaurant, or at a park.

2. Use the checklist on the Total Communication Makeover clipboard to launch your discussion. (Don't feel like you have to do them in order. See how many you make it through in an hour.)

3. If you feel like there's a lot left unsaid, schedule a second date to finish your discussion.

Starter Checklist for a Total Communication Makeover

❑ **Money**—Do you feel you have enough? Do you like how you are spending it? Saving it? What would you do differently?

❑ **Sex**—Frequency? Enjoyable? What do you wish was different?

❑ **Children**—What is the #1 issue right now? What are you praying for? One way to improve your relationship?

❑ **Dreams**—Where would you like to be in five years? In twenty years?

❑ **Church**—Happy with your contribution? What would you change?

❑ **Work**—Satisfying? Too much? Need a change?

❑ **Priorities**—Are they in the right order? What needs adjusting?

❑ **The future**—What needs to be done now for next year? For kid's schooling? For retirement?

❑ **Family vacations**—Memorable? Fun? What would you do differently?

❑ **Parents/In-Laws**—Enough time? Appropriate relationships? What needs to change?

Section 6: Goal

You never know what might happen if you keep praying the Marriage Prayer.

Father,

I said, "'Til death do us part"—I want to mean it.

Help me love You more than him,

and him more than anyone or anything else.

Help me bring him into Your presence today.

Make us one, like You are three in one.

I want to hear him, support him, and serve him—

so he would love You more and we can bring You glory.

Amen.

Goal

The final chapter is about our Goal. Unless something out of the ordinary happens, you and your spouse will likely be married for a long time. That means it's important to know where you are heading and how to stay on track.

In our final chapter, we'll flesh out the following big idea:

▶ **Because I want to finish strong, I'm going to pray The Marriage Prayer every day.**

Praying The Marriage Prayer encapsulates the lessons we've learned in this book. Hopefully God has reinforced and amplified these truths in your heart and mind.

There is no way we can stay on track in our own strength—that's why it's part of the Marriage Prayer. Begin each day asking God to keep you on the path— "So he would love You more and we can bring You glory."

Time-out there, Honey. Don't even think of finishing the last chapter if you aren't praying The Marriage Prayer every day. Am I going to have to bring you down to the principal's office?

11: Finishing Strong
Your Heart and The Marriage Prayer

If the Lord wills and you live to be eighty, how long will you have been married? At that time, if you could choose any words to characterize your marriage, what would you want them to be? (Pick two.)

Her	Him
❑ Joyful	❑ Joyful
❑ Steady	❑ Steady
❑ Exciting	❑ Exciting
❑ Reliable	❑ Reliable
❑ Faithful	❑ Faithful
❑ Thrilling	❑ Thrilling
❑ Romantic	❑ Romantic
❑ Christ-centered	❑ Christ-centered
❑ Adventurous	❑ Adventurous
❑ Fulfilling	❑ Fulfilling
❑ Other _____	❑ Other _____
❑ Other _____	❑ Other _____

RULES OF ENGAGEMENT

Find a quiet place and sit down with your spouse. Tell each other why you chose your words. How well do you think those same words characterize your marriage now?

A (Slightly Disguised) True Story about…Finishing Strong
Joe and Ruth

As she and Joe got ready to leave, Ruth leaned on her cane and chuckled at the conversation going on between their out-of-town guests. Rick had forgotten where he put the car keys, and his wife, Lisa, was grilling him up one side and down the other. "How many times do I have to tell you to keep those keys in your pocket? If they were in your pocket we wouldn't have to look for them." Rick looked like a lost dog, standing in the middle of the room trying to remember where he'd placed the keys.

Ruth stepped back into the living room. "Don't worry about it. My sweet Joe and I will help you look. You two are only in your mid seventies—you're just getting started losing things. We've had a lot more practice."

At eighty-eight and eighty-six, Joe and Ruth have seen a lot during their years, and they know a lot about what it takes to get along with one another. But it wasn't always that way.

For their time, Joe and Ruth got married relatively late—he was thirty and she was twenty-eight. By then, Joe had already established a pattern of drinking and partying that he brought straight into their marriage. If you could have seen them after ten years, you would have concluded their marriage didn't have a chance.

To be continued…

That's a lot of years together.

Your marriage is a precious link in a sacred chain that stretches all the way back to Adam and Eve. Inaugurated by God Himself in the garden of Eden, marriage gives men and women the privilege of stewarding God's creation. The family is a primary unit for accomplishing God's will on earth (Psalm 78). That's why it's so important to finish strong—so you don't break that sacred chain.

Many married couples have lowered their expectations for their marriages too far. These couples have forgotten how sacred and holy marriage really is. God has ordained the two of you to be His representatives in your sphere of influence!

We hope that working through this book has helped you see what God's desire for marriage is all about. That's why we've been praying each day, "So she (or he) would love You more and we can bring You glory."

Having a godly marriage is not just an optional thing that you can choose to pursue or not. The Bible says that the state of our marriage is absolutely critical to the state of our souls. Consider these two passages:

> *Another thing you do: You flood the LORD's altar with tears. You weep and wail because he no longer pays attention to your offerings or accepts them with pleasure from your hands. You ask, "Why?" It is because the LORD is acting as the witness between you and the wife of your youth, because you have broken faith with her, though she is your partner, the wife of your marriage covenant. Has not the LORD made them one? In flesh and spirit they are his. And why one? Because he was seeking godly offspring. So guard yourself in your spirit, and do not break faith with the wife of your youth.* (Malachi 2:13–15)

The state of your marriage both reflects and affects the state of your relationship with God.

> *Husbands, in the same way be considerate as you live with your wives, and treat them with respect as the weaker partner and as heirs with you of the gracious gift of life, so that nothing will hinder your prayers.* (1 Peter 3:7)

Wow! Even our prayers are hinged to the state of our marriages.

PLEASE DO TRY THIS AT HOME

In general, do you think you take your marriage as seriously as God does? Has working through this book helped change your perspective, and if so, how?

Finishing Strong Day by Day

One of the struggles in marriage is that it is so **daily**. And **relentless**. When you woke up this morning your spouse was lying in bed beside you. And that person will be there tomorrow. And the next day. And the day after that. Does that thought make you jump for joy?

It can, but it's hard to finish strong without lots of little decisions to keep you heading in the right direction.

Imagine you are taking a trip and using a compass. For a short hike, if you made an error at the start and read the compass incorrectly by one degree, after one hundred yards you would only be five feet away from your target. However, if you flew a plane six hundred miles with the same one degree error, at the end of your trip you would be ten miles from your destination. (And from where we live in Orlando, a trip to San Diego would end thirty-two miles off target!)

It's the same way in your marriage. If you lose focus and get off track for a little bit, things might seem okay for a matter of days or weeks. But over a period of ten, twenty, or forty years, being off track a little can devastate your marriage. It's as if the two of you left Orlando for San Diego, but one of you ended up south of Tijuana. You'd end up in two countries with two languages separated by border guards! You don't want to get to that point in your marriage.

How to Stay on Track for the Long Run

We've given you a lot of practical steps in this book, because when things aren't working it's important to change the trajectory right away. But we've also tried to help change your belief system. Because in the long-term, **the only thing that will make the Marriage Prayer a reality is God transforming your heart every day.**

A famous experiment was conducted at Stanford University in the 1960s by researcher Walter Mitchell. His team took four-year-old children into a small room one at a time, sat them down and put a marshmallow on the table. The instructor told the child, "I'm going to leave the room right now. If you want to eat the marshmallow, you can, but if you wait until I come back, I'll give you another marshmallow. So instead of having just one marshmallow, you'll have two." Then they left the room for between five and fifteen minutes. As soon as the researcher left, some children grabbed the marshmallow and ate it. Other children held out for a while, but finally went ahead. Some children waited the whole time and received two marshmallows when the researcher came back in the room.

The researchers followed up with these students in elementary school, high school, and after graduation. They found that those who waited and received two marshmallows consistently performed higher throughout those years. This simple test was an incredible predictor of success in life.

Okay. Four-year-olds and marshmallows. How does that connect to marriage?

That insight affects marriage because it demonstrates something about being made in the image of God. The children who were patient and thought long term were more successful. God is also patient and thinks long term. He has ultimate goals in mind and keeps ultimate things ultimate. So, when we give ultimate things priority we reflect His image and glory.

Think about it. Everybody admires people who set goals and sacrifice. We celebrate athletes who train for a long time, or who overcome great obstacles. Remember bicyclist Lance Armstrong? One year as he competed in the Tour de France in June, the commentators mentioned over and over that on a rainy, 42 degree day in March, he rode a thirty-mile climb when most of his competitors were in the hotel getting a massage. We look at that and say, "There's something admirable about that."

Why? Because it is a dim reflection of God's devotion to ultimate things. Our goal in this book has been to help you build your allegiance to ultimate things in marriage.

What are the ultimate things God has for you in your marriage? **To help your spouse love God more, and to bring Him glory.** Everything else really needs to fall in line behind this. That's why every day we have been praying, "So he would love You more and we can bring You glory."

A (Slightly Disguised) True Story about... Finishing Strong
Joe and Ruth (continued)

At year ten of their marriage, Ruth and Joe were living much the same as many of their peers. He worked hard and was building a successful business. They had two young children. Ruth had her own work and a variety of interests in the community. But inside the walls of the house things were different.

Almost every night, Joe would drink the night away in the recliner. Many times Ruth would fix him one more drink and bring it to him, knowing it would be the one that would finally knock him out.

Not a great recipe for finishing strong.

Joe went fishing every weekend with a buddy, but it was basically an excuse to drink beer. Over the next ten years, he and Ruth drifted so far apart they were basically just living together.

Then, about twenty years into their marriage, a couple invited Ruth and Joe to their house on a Friday night for a Bible study. Joe's

still not sure why they went—but they did. And they kept going back.
A few month's later, when Joe was fifty years old, both Ruth and he
asked Christ to forgive their sins and give them new life.

To be continued...

We'd be glad to...

Finish Strong by Being Intentional. We live in a fallen world. Left to its own, everything degrades and deteriorates: your lawn, your garage, your appearance or your marriage. Translation? If you are not intentional you will end up with a mess on your hands.

Don't fall into the trap of going along with the strong currents flowing through your life. Live life, don't let life live you. Not having a plan **is** a plan—for mediocrity at best and failure at worst. Make concrete changes based on what you've read in this book. Don't let it end just because you finish this chapter. Hopefully, you've set some new patterns in motion that will change your marriage for years to come.

Finish Strong by Investing in Your Marriage and One Another. One man told us, "I finally realized that if I lost everything and had to sleep under a bridge, there is only one person who would still be with me." We started the book with this big idea: "After God, but before all others, make your spouse your top priority." That's a great reminder to bring up here at the end.

Find ways to invest in one another. Erica began to play tennis in her mid-thirties and loved it. She asked Rick if he would play mixed doubles with her. Rick had never really played tennis, but eventually he agreed so he could spend more time with Erica. Now they love playing tennis together. (Some men have asked Rick to play matches with them and he just laughs. He still only plays tennis to spend time with Erica.)

Finish Strong by Finding Ways to Give Yourselves Away Together. Successful couples do ministry together. They invest in a mission or cause. It's easy for couples to do all their volunteer work in different areas, especially when the kids are home. He coaches the baseball team, she works with the children's ministry at church.

But you should also consider some outlets to use your gifts together. God made you to "tend the garden" with each other. There are lessons you will learn by doing ministry together that you can't learn any other way.

Tim and Susan used to go their separate ways at church every week. She'd work with children; he'd work with special-needs adults. Now, they are doing marriage ministry together and mentoring young couples. They've seen how God uses their individual gifts together to make them more effective than they ever could have been on their own.

Finish Strong by Having a Sense of Humor. Don't take life too seriously. It's a vapor, then it's gone. Laugh at yourself and at the funny situations life brings. This following true scene illustrates the choice we all face...

The Setting: The not-too-distant past, a few years before online airline reservations, in the Delk's living room.

The Background: David got a call on a Wednesday night telling him that a Man in the Mirror faculty member scheduled for an event that weekend couldn't go. David needed to take his place. We pick up the scene after David has called a major airline and requested tickets from Orlando to Grand Rapids for the following Friday. He speaks to an Airline Person (A.P.).

A.P.:   "I'll look that up. Can you hold for a moment?"

David: "Sure."

A.P.:   "Okay, you can leave Orlando at 6:10 a.m., connect in Cincinnati at 8:40, connect through Salt Lake City at 11:00, and arrive at..."

At this point, David suspects something is wrong. He's no geography expert, but he's pretty sure you shouldn't be stopping in Salt Lake City to get from Orlando to Grand Rapids.

David: "Did you say Salt Lake City? I need to go through Salt Lake City to get to Grand Rapids, Michigan?"

A.P.: "Oh, I thought you said Rapid City. Hold on one moment."

David waits. Finally she comes back on the line and gives him the correct itinerary.

David: "Sounds good. I'll take it. Here's my credit card number."

A.P.: "I'm sorry, sir—it's too close to your departure date. I can't sell you the ticket on the phone. You'll have to go to a ticket office and purchase it."

David is stunned. After clarifying there was no way he can buy the ticket now over the phone, David asks if he can put a hold on the ticket.

A.P.: "Yes, I can hold it but I can't guarantee the price when you actually buy it."

David's wife, Ruthie, enters stage left and takes a seat on the couch to hear the rest of what happens.

David: "Perhaps we still have a misunderstanding. I have my credit card right here and you're saying I can't buy a ticket?"

A.P.: "Actually, sir, there is a way. But I'll have to transfer you and you'll have to pay $75 to gain elite status and then you can make the purchase."

David: (in dismay) "The only way I can purchase this ticket over the phone is to pay you $75 and be transferred..."

A.P.: (cutting David off) "I'm sorry that I cannot help you sir."

Add sound effect of Airline Person hanging up on customer.

As the scene comes to a close, David has a choice.

He can take the phone he is holding and throw it through the wall. (That seems like a surprisingly good idea right now.)

Or he can take a deep breath, and laugh…

And that's what David and Ruthie did. (It helped that she was sitting on the couch chuckling during the second half of the conversation.)

They joked that they were the only people in America who could get hung up on by a major corporation when they were trying to spend $500. (By the way, David called the airline back, spoke to another person, and had his ticket in five minutes.)

Life is filled with funny moments if you look for them.

Make humor a part of your marriage. Watch funny movies. Find a funny friend and say, "Hey, we read this book that said we needed to laugh as part of our marriage—do you mind if we come over for dinner tonight?" Do whatever it takes to laugh together.

Finish Strong by Making Your Marriage a Matrix for Becoming like Christ. Your marriage should be the first and steadiest place of spiritual growth in your life. Christ's love for the church brings transformation so that she can be presented to God holy and blameless. Husbands are to love their wives like Christ loves the church. Wives are supposed to respect their husbands. Here's what this means: God gives us a ministry with our spouses to help them become all they can be.

Finish Strong by Constantly Surrendering Your Own Heart to Christ. The Christian life is a surrendered life. And a Christian marriage is a surrendered marriage.

We need to make one thing perfectly clear. We've given you lots of steps, exercises, and practical ideas in this book. Those are good things to do. But it's not self-effort that will help you finish strong. It's not trying harder, resolving to do better, or making a plan and working the plan. Self-reliance, even in good things, leads to a lifestyle of living independently from God.

God calls us into moment-by-moment surrender. Rather than doing the right things in our own strength, we should do them by faith in Christ. We are to rely on Him by faith for our health, our money, our children, our spouse, our future, our safety, our friendships, and our careers. The only strength in our life that matters is His strength; the only righteousness that matters is the righteousness of Christ produced in us by His Spirit; the only love that matters is the sacrificial love He produces in us.

Through the gospel, we have real spiritual power to see transformation in our lives and the lives of those around us. Don't settle for half hearted or mediocre Christianity. Turn daily to Christ by faith and ask God to do something great in your heart and the heart of your spouse.

Finish Strong by Praying The Marriage Prayer Every Day

All these ideas for finishing strong are elaborations on concepts found in the prayer we introduced in the beginning of this book. That's why we have been emphasizing for you to pray that prayer on a daily basis. We know of nothing better to help you finish strong.

The **Big** Idea

Because I want to finish strong, I'm going to pray The Marriage Prayer every day.

A (Slightly Disguised) True Story about…Finishing Strong
Joe and Ruth (continued)

It took a while for Joe and Ruth to learn what it meant to have a Christian marriage. They hadn't been communicating much at all for the previous ten years of their marriage, so it was a new experience. They started investing in each other. Joe worked hard to connect with Ruth spiritually and reestablish an emotional bond.

They got involved in church as well. It was natural for both of them to share about the transformation that Jesus brought in their lives. So they started talking to friends, neighbors, and visitors at church and saw many people become Christians.

Ruth began hosting Bible studies in their home with women, and Joe began meeting with other men. They found places to serve together where they could have an impact. God had transformed their hearts from the inside out.

They built a marriage that could last.

Now in their later years, they are experiencing God's blessing as they finish strong together. They face health challenges and daily uncertainty about the future. But they still pray together every Wednesday and Saturday morning. They love the visits they receive from people to whom they ministered over the years. Most of all they are thankful to God for rescuing them and giving them a marriage that has thrived through the test of time.

Connection Point

The exercise at the start of this chapter asked you to consider the words you would hope would characterize your marriage if you live to be eighty. Are you making progress? Do those words better characterize your marriage now than they did two years ago? Why? If the rest of your marriage was like the last three months, would you end up where you want to be? Why or why not?

Today is the day to make changes so you can become the couple God has called you to be. Your marriage can be a shining example of the grace and goodness of Jesus Christ. There can be a day when people could look at your marriage and say, "Only God could help people love like that."

Isn't that the kind of marriage you want to have, for the glory of God? Our hope is that The Marriage Prayer will open your heart and mind to the power of Christ every day.

CHAPTER REVIEW

Don't stop praying The Marriage Prayer every day just because you've come to the end of this book! Let's see how well prepared you are to keep going. Fill in the blanks for the missing words. Give yourself 10 points for every blank you get correct.

For Him

Father,

I said, "'Til _____ do us part"–I want to _____ it.

Help me _____ _____ more than _____,

    and her more than anyone or _____ else.

Help me _____ her into Your _____ today.

_____ us one, like You are _____ in _____.

I want to _____ her, _____ her, and _____ her–

so she would _____ You more and we can bring You _____.

Amen.

For Her

Father,

I said, "'Til _____ do us part"–I want to _____ it.

Help me _____ _____ more than _____,

    and him more than _____ or anything else.

Help me _____ him into Your _____ today.

_____ us _____, like You are three in one.

I want to _____ him, _____ him, and serve him–

so he would _____ You more and we can _____ You _____.

Amen.

You Haven't Finished This Chapter Until...

This is your last chance. Let God finish the work that He wants to do in your heart. Finishing strong can bring incredible joy; blowing it can bring unbelievable pain.

So, please don't lay this book aside until...

❑ You've completed the exercises, including the Please Do Try This at Home (p. 200) and the Connection Point (p. 208)

❑ You have cemented the habit of praying The Marriage Prayer every day.

❑ With your spouse and/or a group, you've discussed the reflection questions.

Questions for Reflection and Discussion

1. What aspects of marriage do you think will bring you the greatest joy as you finish strong? Share these ideas with your spouse.

2. Which parts of the "True Story" connect with your experience so far? What lessons are there in the story that might apply to your life?

3. The big idea tells us to pray The Marriage Prayer. Have you been doing that? What difference has it made in your life?

4. What application will you take away from this chapter? What's your plan to finish strong?

A One-Hour Deposit for the Heart
Section 6: Goal

For weeks, you've been praying "So she (he) would love Your more and we can bring You glory." Here is a practical way to help this goal become even more of a reality in your marriage. Plan a time when you can spend about an hour alone together.

1. Begin by finding a wedding picture, looking through your wedding album, or just examining your wedding rings. Each of you take a minute or two to consider the following questions silently, then discuss.

   ■ What are one or two of your favorite memories from your wedding day?

   ■ What were some of your dreams when you got married? (What kind of house did you imagine living in? How many kids? How much money? What kind of career(s)?)

2. Consider your marriage and life at the present time. Reflect on these questions individually for a moment, then discuss.

   ■ How have your dreams for your marriage worked out?

   ■ In what ways has it been more a struggle?

   ■ In what ways has your life been better than you expected?

3. To finish strong, you should look for ways to give yourselves away as a couple for the glory of God. Think about these questions individually for a couple of minutes, then talk about them together.

   ■ What are some ways you are serving for the glory of God today?

   ■ How have you had the most fun in the past serving God? Where do you think you've had the greatest impact?

   ■ What is one opportunity you might enjoy doing at some point as a couple? When could that become a reality, and how?

Close your time together with pray. Pray The Marriage Prayer, and also pray that God would help you finish strong in your marriage by continuing to pursue Him and one another with your whole hearts.

Group Leader's Guide

It's easy to start a group to discuss *The Marriage Prayer*. Here's a step-by-step guide…

Starting a Group

Share a copy of this book with a few couples with whom you might want to meet. Alternatively, copy the table of contents and the discussion questions from the end of a few chapters. Ask them if they would like to be in a group to read and discuss the material. This can be a group from your work, church, neighborhood or a combination. Invite anyone you would like. The optimum size for the group would be four to six couples.

When You First Meet

The first week together, give a copy of the book and a schedule of your upcoming meetings to each couple. Assign the introductory material and the first chapter as next week's reading assignment. Ask them to work through the exercises and to talk at the meeting next week about the discussion questions at the end of the chapter.

Then go around the room and ask each couple to share with the group where they are on their spiritual pilgrimage. This is a great icebreaker, and the couples will be encouraged to hear one another's stories. Be sure to point out that there are no wrong answers to this question. Some many just be starting on their pilgrimage; others may be well down the road. Close with a prayer. Always adjourn exactly when you said you would.

Typical Week

After giving folks a chance to say hi and reconnect, begin by asking if any couple wants to share their reaction to an exercise in this week's chapter. Was there a question or exercise that prompted a particularly interesting discussion? Why?

Then read through and talk about the Questions for Reflection and Discussion at the end of the chapter.

Here's a good schedule for a ninety-minute meeting:

- Ten minutes for icebreaker/fellowship
- Sixty minutes for discussion questions
- Twenty minutes for group prayer
- End promptly at the scheduled time.

Leading the Discussion

The best groups are facilitated by shepherds, not teachers. Don't feel as if you have to have all the answers. Rather, your role is to encourage each couple to share their thoughts. Try to make sure everyone in the group gets some "air time." If someone dominates the time, privately ask them to help you draw out the more reserved members of the group. And remember, it's more important to talk about "real" things than it is to answer every single question.

Experience

You don't have to be an experienced Bible teacher to lead a discussion. If someone asks a question beyond your scope, simply say so and move on.

The Next Step

You have created momentum with the couples in your group. Don't finish the study without capturing this momentum. After the fifth or sixth week, begin to let them know your next steps and how they can stay involved. If you will not continue as a group, make sure you take them to an alternative opportunity (another group, class at your church, etc.) and help them make the transition. Your role is not complete until your couples have successfully taken these next steps.

For more information on discipleship processes in the local church, visit www.maninthemirror.org, where you will find dozens of leadership training and small-group materials and over five hundred free resources.

Chapter Review Answer Key

Chapter 1: 1) b, 2) c, 3) b, 4) c

Chapter 2: See The Marriage Prayer on page 16.

Chapter 3: priority, vulnerability, honest, plan, unforgiveness, self-focus

Chapter 4: romance, cherish, tender, connection, respect

Chapter 5:

Chapter 6:

Chapter 7: oneness, representation, one flesh, pull apart, draw together, other-centered, investing time, charity, gift-love, pursuit, When God sees you and your spouse He sees one flesh

Chapter 8: 1) d,   2) c,   3) b,   4) b

Chapter 9:

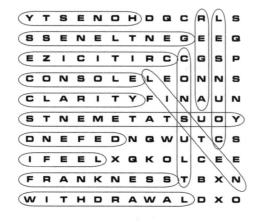

Chapter 10: credit, marketing, investment, retirement, promises

Chapter 11: See The Marriage Prayer on page 17.

Additional Resources

Devotionals

Patrick Morley, *Devotions for Couples*. Grand Rapids: Zondervan, 2000.

H. Norman Wright, *Quiet Times for Couples*. Eugene, Oreg.: Harvest House, 1997.

Books for Men Who Want to be Better Husbands

Patrick Morley, *The Man in the Mirror*. Grand Rapids: Zondervan, 2000.

Shaunti and Jeff Feldhahn, *For Men Only*. Sisters, Oreg.: Multnomah, 2006.

Larry Crabbe, *The Silence of Adam*. Grand Rapids: Zondervan, 1998.

Patrick Morley, *A Man's Guide to the Spiritual Discipliness*. Chicago: Moody, 2007.

Books for Women Who Want to be Better Wives

Patrick Morley, *What Husbands Wish Their Wives Knew About Men*. (Free e-book, www.maninthemirror.org/rc/ebooks.htm.)

Shaunti Feldhahn, *For Women Only*. Sisters, Oreg: Multnomah, 2004.

Paula Rinehart, *Strong Women, Soft Hearts*. Nashville: W Publishing, 2005.

Overcoming Addictions or Abuse

Edward T. Welch, *Addictions: A Banquet in the Grave*. Phillipsburg, N.J.: P&R Publishing, 2001.

Mark Laaser, *Faithful and True Workbook*. Nashville: LifeWay, 1999.

Dan B. Allender, *The Wounded Heart* Colorado Springs: NavPress, 1995.

Summary of All Big Ideas

1. After God, but before all others, make your spouse your top priority.

2. It is God's will for this marriage to work.

3. We resolve conflict well when we exchange our natural self-focus for a God-and-spouse focus.

4. Romance blooms when I cherish my spouse the way God cherishes me.

5. Our marriage will thrive when we both submit to God's divine order.

6. Marriage works well when we worship well.

7. When God sees you and your spouse, He sees "one flesh."

8. Physical intimacy is the by-product of many small sacrifices done with no ulterior motive.

9. Everyone is good at communicating about what is interesting to them.

10. Most people live like money will do what it promises and that God won't do what He promises.

11. Because I want to finish strong. I'm going to pray The Marriage Prayer every day.

Are you interested in reaching men in your church and community?

Man in the Mirror can give you the tools, strategy, and encouragement you need to help you be more effective in evangelizing and discipling men.

Serving Leaders in the Battle for Men's Souls

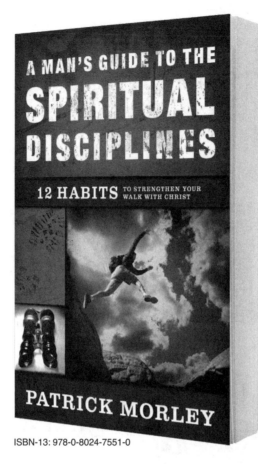

ISBN-13: 978-0-8024-7551-0

For every ten men in church, nine will have children who leave the church. Eight will not find their jobs satisfying. Six will pay only the monthly minimum on their credit card balances. Five will have a major problem with pornography. Four will get divorced (affecting one million children per year). Only one will have a biblical worldview, and all ten will wrestle to balance work and family. With these kinds of issues facing men today, we need more than an annual men's gathering and regular church attendance to keep our faith strong. It takes discipline and determination to stand against the tide. *A Man's Guide to the Spiritual Disciplines* will give men the tools they need to reflect Christ in the context of marriage, family, and the daily grind. And that's what men are made for.

by Patrick Morley
Find it now at your favorite local or online bookstore.
www.MoodyPublishers.com

Other Tools for Church Leadership include:

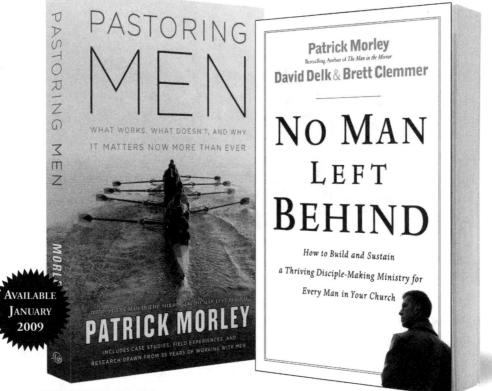